BOTHO STRAUSS
THREE PLAYS

Botho Strauss

THREE PLAYS

THE PARK
SEVEN DOORS
TIME AND THE ROOM

Translated by Jeremy Sams

OBERON BOOKS
LONDON

First published in these translations in 2006 by Oberon Books Ltd
521 Caledonian Road, London N7 9RH
Tel: +44 (0) 20 7607 3637 / Fax: +44 (0) 20 7607 3629
e-mail: info@oberonbooks.com
www.oberonbooks.com

Der Park © Carl Hanser Verlag München Wien 1983

Sieben Türen © Carl Hanser Verlag München Wien 1988

Die Zeit und das Zimmer © Carl Hanser Verlag München Wien 1988

Translations copyright © Jeremy Sams 2004–2006

A catalogue record for this book is available from the British Library.

ISBN: 978-1-84002-476-0

Cover design by Andrzej Klimowski

Visit www.oberonbooks.com to read more about all our books and to buy them. You will also find features, author interviews and news of any author events, and you can sign up for e-newsletters so that you're always first to hear about our new releases.

These translations are dedicated to
Steven Pimlott
who first introduced me to Botho Strauss.

J.S.

Contents

THE PARK

Characters

GEORGE

HELEN

TITANIA

OBERON

FIRSTLING

COURTLING

THREE BOYS

TWO GIRLS

HELMA

BLACK BOY

CYPRIAN

WOLF

DEATH – THE MAN IN BLACK

THREE YOUNG MEN

BARMAN

YOUNG WAITER

TITANIA'S FABLE-SON

WAITRESS

This translation of *The Park* was first produced by the RSC in 1995 at the Pit Theatre, with the following company:

GEORGE, Simon Dormandy

HELEN, Julie Graham

TITANIA, Louise Jameson

OBERON, Adrian Lukis

FIRSTLING, Simon Kunz

COURTLING, Michael Jenn

BOY, Tom Williams

GIRL, Alison Reid

HELMA, Tessa Peake-Jones

BLACK BOY, Garron Mitchell

CYPRIAN, Barry McCarthy

WOLF, Richard Hope

DEATH / FABLE-SON, Jo Stone-Fewings

BARMAN, Tom Walker

YOUNG WAITER, Mark Lutheren

LITTLE MAN, Daniel Sharman

Director & Designer, David Fielding

Lighting Designer, Thomas Webster

Music, Adrian Johnston

Act One

SCENE 1

Town park. Bushes. The red elder twigs are bare, as if in winter. All sorts of rubbish lying around: paper, beer cans, old tights, shoes, a broken cassette trailing tape. While the stage is still dark, headlamps pass over the scene. Sounds of circus animals in their cages. Then light; dull light. We see a sand-pit; the sand is filthy. Behind, a dark red curtain, split down the middle. Strong light shines from this opening. An empty trapeze sways to and fro. HELEN is sitting on the edge of the sand-pit. Shaking. Smoking a cigarette. Enter GEORGE.

GEORGE: Good evening – how's it going?

HELEN: Oh, hi! Well, you know. Not so bad – it's all right – it's okay.

GEORGE: I thought it would be nice to see you again.

I thought I'd…

HELEN: Fine… Great.

GEORGE: So. How's things. How's Art?

HELEN: Art? You're joking, you call that art? What they do isn't art. Art's something else. They're just a bunch of fucking amateurs in there.

GEORGE: Look, you're freezing to death. Why aren't you in rehearsing with the others?

HELEN: Me? I'm not working with that lot any more. No way am I working with them any more.

GEORGE: God, did you have a bust-up with your colleagues? What happened, did you get fed up with them? Did they get fed up with you?

HELEN: With me? Listen, they think I'm fabulous. They're crazy about me. I show up and I say, 'Here, watch this, you'll love this.' And I do them 'Sexy Helen on her Bed of Nails' or 'The Birdwoman'. You know, shit like that. But up on the trapeze it's nothing but nag, nag, nag. My timing isn't right, or I'm too tall, or I'm too short. Always some little gripe. So I start thinking, fuck this, I'm not some dumb little bimbo they can push around the whole time.

GEORGE: I'm sure they'll be missing you in there.

HELEN: They won't... I took a dive.

GEORGE: You what?

HELEN: I fell – from up there – fell off. Fell down...

GEORGE: Off the rope?

HELEN: Off the trapeze.

GEORGE: With a safety net?

HELEN: Nope.

GEORGE: Didn't you hurt yourself?

HELEN: I didn't get right back up there. That's the thing. That's the thing you're not allowed to do. I'm doing this double twist – piece of cake – and then I just kind of fell. Look I can do a double twist, no problem. But this time I missed Pascal's hand. Completely misjudged it. So down I go slap-bang into the sand. And I didn't go back up. I thought, no way are you going back up there. And that's the rule in the circus. You gotta get back up there. Even if it's some amateur outfit. Even then. You've got to do it again or you've blown it for good.

GEORGE: I'll drive you to the hospital. Someone should take a look at you.

HELEN: No. No, leave it. I'll just go and have a wash. Shitty amateur bloody circus. Sheer waste of time. Bunch of no-hopers. Just amateurs. All talk, no action.

GEORGE: Come on. We'll go and have a drink.

HELEN: Really? Okay. Fine.

(*He puts his jacket over her shoulders. They leave.*)

I know these guys, these so-called superstars. I tell you, I'm every bit as good as them. They got nothing on me, none of them. Big mouths, but that's all.

SCENE 2

TITANIA and OBERON's heads appear in the bushes.

TITANIA: Back again, my Oberon? Back
    To pursue your sad, pathetic cause?

OBERON: Do not mock me, heartless Titania.

TITANIA: Me, I am no more heartless than you, my jealous Lord.

OBERON: Not even the clods of mud beneath our feet
    Can temper the pace of your lust.
TITANIA: Nor does your jealousy appear to wane
    Though now it stalks me through the cold, and empty
    Cities, and not, as once it did
    Through the soft meadows of the clouds.
    You hunt me through the heavens and on earth
    But still your jealous song remains the same.
OBERON: Then stay here by my side, and let us try
    To double our effect upon the cities.
    Our endless bickering can only serve
    To dull our radiance.
TITANIA: True, my Oberon
    But still, our love of lust will always make us
    Seem cantankerous.
OBERON: I have nothing against lust, certainly not my own.
TITANIA: No more have I.
    But when you cram a god into this frame,
    This finite insufficient human shape,
    It will hurt. It does, it's bloody agony.
    (*They disappear. Enter FIRSTLING and COURTLING.*)
FIRSTLING: Look, don't be offended, but it's this far and no
    further. This is far enough.
COURTLING: But is this the place? Is it here that it starts?
FIRSTLING: Let's go back, it doesn't feel quite right…
COURTLING: I don't believe this! You're too scared to go
    walking through the park at night and yet you still have
    these dreams, like some randy old bull, of knocking a
    woman down in the bushes and raping her on the spot.
FIRSTLING: The fat woman. Yes, rather.
COURTLING: The fat woman. Who goes around with the
    skinniest man in the world. That beanpole. Legs like
    flamingos.
FIRSTLING: Used to. Used to go around with him. The thin
    man is dead.
COURTLING: No – really?
FIRSTLING: Yes.
COURTLING: Why is he dead?
FIRSTLING: What do you mean, 'why'?

COURTLING: What did he die of?

FIRSTLING: What of? A thin man, who gets thinner every day, sooner or later he's just going to vanish. He died of a wasting disease. A virus. A wasting virus. Probably an unknown virus.

COURTLING: People were always wondering. How is it that this painfully thin, almost non-existent chap comes to be knocking around with a spherical woman? I bet they met through the lonely hearts.

FIRSTLING: One of those video things…

COURTLING: Computer dating!

FIRSTLING: They met in a database.

COURTLING: That always produces such weird couples.

FIRSTLING: The joke couple.

COURTLING: Let's go back.

FIRSTLING: You see, that's what I've been saying all along. We'd best go back.

(They exit. OBERON steps forward, stands near the curtain. Enter FIRST BOY and FIRST GIRL. He is in dungarees; she has thick glasses, torn jogging shoes, T-shirt with Mickey Mouse, jeans torn at the knee, chain round her ankle, painted cheeks, painted knees; a soft toy, a dog, under her arm. They are carrying a case of beer.)

FIRST BOY: We always seem to be out of sync. Why can't you keep in step with me?

FIRST GIRL: No, you keep in with me…

(Exeunt. Enter HELMA. TITANIA opens her coat, exposes herself. HELMA stares, terrified at the white body, like a statue, its underbelly covered with thick hair, like an animal. She then runs to OBERON.)

HELMA: *(To OBERON.)* Excuse me, sorry but over there in the bushes…a woman. I mean…I've never seen anything like it. Disgusting. There's this woman…exposing herself. Thick hair, like an animal. She just opened her coat – God it gave me such a shock. Would you call the police? I mean, there could be children about, children could see it.

OBERON: I know a bank where the wild thyme blows
Where oxlips and the nodding violet grows
Quite overcanopied with luscious woodvine

With sweet musk-roses and with eglantine.
There sleeps Titania some time of the night,
Lulled in these flowers with dances and delight
And there the snake throws her enamelled skin…
(*He exposes himself. Exit HELMA.*)

SCENE 3

TITANIA: You didn't get very far with her, my Lord.

OBERON: Nor did you.

TITANIA: She stood in front of me a little longer.

She took a longer look at me…

OBERON: The seed of the moment is sown,

We must wait and watch it 'til it's grown.

TITANIA: I can't help feeling that we're doing something wrong.

When we display ourselves – they're far from thrilled.

I've yet to see a face light up with joy,

Or a single spark that's mirrored back at me.

I need that sweet reflection of our light,

However weak, however human – it would give me

Strength.

They just walk past me, gloomily, or worse

They scream at me, appalled. Is that desire?

Do they have any sex in them at all?

OBERON: The human race knows nothing of desire.

Nothing of the force with which other beings on other

Stars collide and conjoin. Their unions are

The palest imitation of our own

And what they see as sensual excess

Seems pathetic, bungled, a trickle not a flood.

Their sense of pleasure is to ours as a lizard

Is to a dragon.

And now the feeble little flame they have

Is flickering and threatens to go out.

Unless we can incite them to new urges,

New desires.

TITANIA: But how?

Here on earth you can make but

The briefest display

Of your undiminished self.
Any more would burn them up.
Your powers are restricted
You cannot be a god on earth.
And meanwhile we are stuck down here
Two unwelcome missionaries in the bushes.

OBERON: But I see the need in so many faces
I hear the things they cannot say.
In the end we'll bring them to their senses
I feel it – I'm sure they'll soon be ready for us.
Their instincts have been so eroded by
Self-consciousness and the need to make a living
That some are even turning
To the ancient gods for help.
And we must get there first,
Be the first to wake their deeper urges
And melt their frozen crust of self-control
And if it works, if we *can* reach them, then
As long as there is life on earth
Then we will be worshipped and adored
And all the rich rewards will come to us
And not to those who follow after.

TITANIA: And we won't be stuck here in the shrubbery, like
A pair of grim old flashers,
Cursed to be endlessly exposing ourselves to an
Unenthusiastic world!

OBERON: You must be patient, my Titania.
Ordinary tax-payers won't pen love-songs
Overnight.
And we're hardly likely to find the legendary lust
Of King Solomon in a driving instructor.
For the time being I can only hope to sow
Confusion among them. And when at last their
Dull souls begin to glow, only then will we
Start to see our own soft reflections in their eyes.
I long for it – and so do you.
I cannot do without it for much longer.

TITANIA: Hush – who comes here?

OBERON: It is your black boy, Titania.

With Cyprian, the artist, in hot pursuit.

TITANIA: Your artist is a bore, Oberon.

And I wish he wouldn't follow my new friend around
The whole time.

(*Enter the BLACK BOY in the overalls of a park-cleaner. He's
pushing a little trolley, collecting rubbish. Behind him, CYPRIAN,
about sixty, in a grey smock. He has a high brow, a gaunt face,
a strong curly head of hair.*)

CYPRIAN: Norman; Kekou!… Spare me a moment *please*.

(*BLACK BOY shakes his head.*)

What, then?

(*BLACK BOY shrugs.*)

Won't you come and see me? You *did* promise…

(*BLACK BOY exits.*)

What can she do that's so special? Okay she can produce
white shirts out of the earth. Big deal. I can make masks,
statues, things you'd like. Just things, though. Things
which you don't want to look at. Oh Titania of the Moon,
you're stealing from a beggar – you should be ashamed of
yourself. And you, you unutterable beauty, you haven't
even got the guts to tell her that you still, sometimes, find
an old man…rather charming.

Every day we used to go for walks…

And now today I've gone and hurt my foot…

There in the bushes – filthy, sick and bare…

I see beyond the dark unknown

I see the light behind their eyes

The hollow King has found his throne

A heap of rats piled to the skies.

(*He exits. Enter SECOND BOY and SECOND GIRL. They sit.*)

SECOND BOY: There are people who want to be on their own
and don't know how. And then people who haven't got
any choice. I don't know which you are…

SECOND GIRL: I want to.

SECOND BOY: Hmmm…

SECOND GIRL: I tell you what I think's wrong, that's when
people won't even admit there's a problem.

SECOND BOY: Yeah that's the worst thing you can do.

SECOND GIRL: Or when they go off on a cruise, say…

SECOND BOY: Yuck!

SECOND GIRL: I s'pose they think, you know, there'll be loads of people around.

SECOND BOY: Gross!

SECOND GIRL: Yeah. You're with all these people all the time, but you can't get away from your own problems. I mean the problems you have relating to other people…

SECOND BOY: But if you really want to find out…the truth. Then why don't you go and spend six months or so in Finland. You know, way up north. A little wood hut with a sauna. By yourself.

SECOND GIRL: Too many mosquitoes.

SECOND BOY: Well…depends…

SECOND GIRL: Who wants to be swatting and scratching all day?

SECOND BOY: Look, for people like us there'll always be, you know, whether we're in Finland or anywhere, there'll alway be this problem that'll never go away. And actually there's no point in even talking about it – that's human sexuality.

SECOND GIRL: Well, I dunno. S'pose so…

SECOND BOY: Go on, be honest. Be absolutely honest.

SECOND GIRL: I am honest.

SECOND BOY: Yeah, right…

SECOND GIRL: I don't see how you can possibly know whether I'm honest or not.

SECOND BOY: We're the same sort of people, you and I. I know you, I know all your tricks.

SECOND GIRL: If you know me you must know I don't have any tricks.

SECOND BOY: Oh God what's the point? I wouldn't want to be you. Not if I was on my own. Being on your own? You don't know the basics.

(*Exeunt. TITANIA is discovered with the BLACK BOY.*)

OBERON: What are you doing, what are you doing?
You're destroying the image, destroying the light.
Come on, get up…

TITANIA: You only want the glory, to be worshipped by mankind.
You lock me up inside this cage of bones.

You make me suffer. And I want to go back home.
Back to my wide, and endless meadows.

OBERON: You're here to be a holy apparition.

Not to *fraternise*...

You'll cease to be Titania of the Moon.

And lose all your dark powers if you acquire

The habit of imperfect human love.

TITANIA: Yes, yes, Oberon, yes. Stop hurting me.

(*Enter FIRST BOY.*)

OBERON: Destroying our image, splintering our light.

And that is all the power that we have.

(*She escapes OBERON, runs to FIRST BOY.*)

TITANIA: (*To FIRST BOY.*)

Excuse me sir, could you tell me the time?

(*She kisses his hand.*)

I've been waiting for you for so long. You're

The one, take me away – take me with you!

OBERON: Stop her.

That's just her way.

It'll pass.

Thanks a lot.

(*FIRST BOY exits.*)

TITANIA: I've had enough.

I know the score

I see it all.

Only death knows more than I do

I want to go home.

Where we are understood – and where things *work*.

OBERON: Listen to me, Titania. Listen well.

We *will* go home – not when we want it,

But only when their eyes are opened.

Only when their weary mortal souls are

Suffused with our image, and awake.

Only when they find desire again

Only then will we be released from this

Ungainly, ugly incarnation

And then our spirits will be free to reign

As unrestricted as in fairy land.

But here your kingdom will be vaster still

If you can stay here patient by my side
And be an inspiration to the world
Holy, happy and uncorrupted
As long as you can leave that black boy alone,
Who belongs to my servant Cyprian.
You harass and confuse him with your ways
Instead of making him rejoice…
The weary coldness and the futile pride
Which you produce within him, are they not
The very things we came here to dispel,
The bitterest enemies to our mission?

TITANIA: Yes, my Oberon.

OBERON: Then listen well.
Renounce your influence upon that boy
And give him back to me.
And I will show him the true stuff of passion.
And give him to my servant Cyprian,
To reward him for his service.

TITANIA: Yes, my Oberon.

OBERON: You're always saying 'yes'
And then you do the opposite.
This coldness in the world is not my fault.
Nor am I to blame for the full moon no longer drives
Men mad.
Nor that the hot midsummer's night no longer
Turns lovers into lunatics.
God knows there's no shortage of lunatics.
But their madness seems turned inwards
As they weep and wail over their own shortcomings.
But who becomes mad for someone else?
(*Enter THIRD BOY.*)
No, my Queen, the fault lies in us –
In our desire, in our dissension.
And that is why we cannot please the world.

TITANIA: (*Bored, reluctant.*) Hi! Excuse me, have you got the…?

THIRD BOY: Sure, it's…

OBERON: No. Don't do it. Please be quiet.

TITANIA: I've been waiting for you for so long…
(*Exit THIRD BOY.*)

OBERON: The time? Why on earth do *you* want to know the
time?

TITANIA: I need to know.

OBERON: You don't need to know the time!

TITANIA: I do. I have to find out.

OBERON: My words are all in vain.

TITANIA: It's getting dark
   And by my pinewoods the twilit lakes
   Will be winking sweetly at the sky.
   I'd go and lie upon my mossy bed,
   And elves would softly sing me to my rest
   Now I have to stretch out on a concrete bench.
   The only songs I hear are fire alarms and car-horns.
   Farewell. 'Til a better time than this.
   (*She exits.*)

OBERON: Well go your way.
   I know how to make you change your mind.
   You shall not endanger our cause,
   And your stubborn pride will not prevail for long.
   I know other ways. Not those of your elves,
   Your sprites, your flower fairies,
   Other ways to tame your impudence and to bend
   Your will to mine.
   I will find a suitable torment for you.
   Cyprian, Cyprian! Can you hear me?

CYPRIAN: (*Sleepily.*) Yes.

OBERON: It is time.
   Time for you to make your masterpiece.

CYPRIAN: I'm afraid… I'm afraid…

OBERON: Are you an artist or not?
   (*CYPRIAN shrugs.*)

SCENE 4

*Stage on two levels. Above, GEORGE and HELEN's house. Below, a table
in a café. GEORGE and WOLF in café.*

GEORGE: Can we talk seriously for a bit? You met Helen a
   while back. What d'you make of her?

WOLF: Helen. What does she do? I mean who is she?

GEORGE: Funnily enough, I don't actually know. I can't get her to tell me. Trouble is she lies all the time. She tells these lies, like a little girl. She came into my office about a year and a half ago. She'd got into some sort of phoney marriage with a Lebanese – she got paid for it – to help him get a resident's permit. And now she was trying to get a divorce, to be free to do the same sort of deal again. I looked after her, you know, as a lawyer. I helped her to extricate herself from the whole organised marriage business. She's half-German, half-American. Her mother's still over in the States.

WOLF: You don't seem to have that much in common.

GEORGE: Do you mean you'd feel a bit iffy about my marrying her?

WOLF: Well, you know, one should always be supportive to one's friends' leanings, no matter what strange byways love may lead them down. But, seriously. As far as you and Helen are concerned it's a big step. I mean, it's one's duty to be there for each other.

GEORGE: Duty? That sounds a bit dubious.

WOLF: You know me, George. We don't really need to say any more about it.

GEORGE: No.

(*HELEN and GEORGE in their house.*)

HELEN: You've been with Wolf, haven't you?

GEORGE: Yes.

HELEN: Something on your mind?

GEORGE: No…nothing.

HELEN: What's he think about us, your friend?

GEORGE: Well – he wishes us the very very best.

HELEN: Is that supposed to be ironic, or is that how you talk to each other?

GEORGE: No. Not ironic. Not at all. Dead serious.

HELEN: Did you work out exactly what he thought about us?

GEORGE: You mean about you? What he thinks about you?

HELEN: Yes, of course.

GEORGE: He warned me about marrying you.

HELEN: Ah!

24

GEORGE: He said that, if he were really to follow his instincts then he'd try and talk me out of it.

HELEN: And how do you feel about his 'warning'?

GEORGE: Well of course you understand, when a good friend like Wolf says something like that, then I can't simply ignore it.

HELEN: Not ignore it…? What about *your* own instincts?

(*GEORGE shrugs.*)

I don't get this, I don't get it at all.

(*HELEN and WOLF in the café.*)

Why are you saying such awful things about me? You don't know me.

WOLF: I've never said anything awful about you.

HELEN: You did so; you warned George about me.

WOLF: I did what? Oh come on, on the contrary, I congratulated him on having decided to settle down at last.

HELEN: But he said you said we didn't suit each other.

WOLF: Well, then he's lying. I never said anything of the kind. But to be honest there is something we haven't discussed. Something we can never discuss. You see I can't disguise the fact that you are – obviously, I'm not blind – a very attractive woman. And if you must know I'm jealous of George.

HELEN: Oh I see. Really?

(*HELEN and GEORGE at home.*)

George. I met up with your friend Wolf.

GEORGE: And?

HELEN: He said you'd been pals since university days.

GEORGE: Yes – that's right.

HELEN: What's he doing being a driving instructor?

GEORGE: Well he inherited this driving school. Actually he got a degree in history. Then he took over his father's business.

HELEN: And of course, you were right – he can't stand me.

GEORGE: Aha. What did he say?

HELEN: He doesn't think I'm right for you.

GEORGE: What, he said that to your face?

HELEN: And he'll do anything in his power to stop you, to stop his best friend from making this terrible mistake. I hate his guts.

GEORGE: No. You mustn't. Look obviously it's terribly tricky, such a delicate relationship between three people who…

HELEN: Three? What about Helma? What about his wife?

GEORGE: Yes, of course there's Helma – but that's a different matter. He feels particularly drawn to us.

HELEN: Not to me – to you. I think you're going to have to decide. It's either him or me…

GEORGE: I hardly think it should come to that.

HELEN: Why not? Or you mean you've already decided?

GEORGE: Look. Wolf is my best friend and I'm in love with you. I don't see that there's any connection.

HELEN: Ah but there is. A big one. He doesn't accept me and I won't accept him. So your heart is split down the middle.
(*GEORGE and WOLF in a café.*)

GEORGE: You've never really told me what you think of Helen.

WOLF: Well you obviously sensed it. 'Cause you told her, didn't you, that I didn't think that much of her.

GEORGE: Is that true?

WOLF: Well, since then I've had the opportunity of getting to know her a bit better. Actually I think you're rather well-suited.

GEORGE: What do you mean?

WOLF: I mean I think you should get married – soon.

GEORGE: Is that your subtle way of saying goodbye to me? I won't marry her if it means the end of our relationship.

WOLF: So I'm supposed to admire your wife and still be your best friend. Is that it?

GEORGE: Wolf, look, on the one hand you've got Helma and a well-ordered home life. And on the other you can have this very special spiritual rapport with us, with Helen and me.

WOLF: You mean like one of the family.

GEORGE: Exactly. Be one of us. In a sense. Up to a point.

WOLF: This is what Helen thinks as well?

GEORGE: Of course. She specifically asked me to offer you her friendship – which is, when all is said and done, the same as mine.
(*HELEN and WOLF in the café.*)

WOLF: How can you be so two-faced? Offering me your 'friendship' via George.

HELEN: What? I never did that.

WOLF: Do you really think my feelings for you have anything to do with friendship?

HELEN: I really don't know. All I know is that the thing you want most is to drive me and George apart.

WOLF: Didn't I make my feelings clear to you last time we met? And yet here you are again, back to see me.

HELEN: I came to see you to ask you to leave me and my man alone.

WOLF: Your 'man', however, doesn't seem equally keen to give up his friendship with me. And if you really love George you won't force him to.

HELEN: I can't be married to George *and* his best friend.

WOLF: Well it's not going to come to that.

HELEN: Because you've already managed to split us up!

WOLF: On the contrary, I'd do anything in my power to preserve George's friendship – which is why the two of you will be closer than ever.

HELEN: What do you mean 'in your power'?

WOLF: I mean, for example, I desire you…and that's because there's nothing George wants more – than for me to desire you.

HELEN: His wishes can hardly dictate your feelings…

WOLF: They should be able to. In a husband's eyes, not to mention his arms, his wife's value rises in direct proportion to how much she appeals to his best friend. Sorry to talk about the heart in terms of the stock exchange. He then repays his friend, with interest, by liking him all the more. Which in turn makes the friend fancy the wife even more.

HELEN: The heart is nothing like the stock exchange. What do you want from me?

WOLF: Oh, that's a loaded question!

HELEN: Would you have found me as desirable if you'd met me on your own – not with George?

WOLF: Not really…

HELEN: You're so cynical – it's repulsive. You're no friend to George.

WOLF: You'll learn what a good friend I can be when you permit me to pursue you with a will. Look out – I'll be

27

whispering all sorts of sweet nothings – or rather specific somethings in your ear.

HELEN: I've got no choice but to tell George what you're really like.

(*GEORGE and HELEN at home.*)

Oh by the way, I bumped into your friend Wolf the other day. I think he's a really fascinating guy.

GEORGE: Ah, you see, it worked!

HELEN: What worked?

GEORGE: Okay, I'll come clean. I'm afraid I've been the teeniest bit dishonest. I offered him your friendship. Without your permission obviously. And of course he was delighted to accept.

HELEN: Seems like you like doing things behind my back now and then.

GEORGE: Yes, okay, but look, if it all turns out for the best…and now Wolf thinks you're the best thing since – whatever. And just now you said you thought he was this 'really fascinating guy'. And obviously everything's fine between me and him.

HELEN: Obviously. And between you and me?

GEORGE: Well I don't see how anything could go wrong. Unless your feelings have changed… I mean, look, if everything between you and him is fine, and everything between him and me is fine, then according to the logic of emotion it must therefore follow that everything between you and me is…

Blackout.

Act Two

SCENE 1

In CYPRIAN's studio. A work table, a sofa. Behind, parts of large masks and papier mâché sculptures. Various working materials, amber, beeswax, earth, a microscope, pincers, scalpels etc, a magnifying glass. Various measuring instruments. CYPRIAN is in a grey smock and jeans, holds a tiny statuette in his hand, shows it to WOLF.

CYPRIAN: Pretty wacky, huh? (*Laughs.*)

WOLF: It's like she's alive! She's like a little saint!

> (*CYPRIAN bends down and gets two more figures from under the carpet.*)

CYPRIAN: Tiny, tiny people, huh?

WOLF: Your creations?

CYPRIAN: Measure things, he says. Measure, measure, measure. What am I supposed to measure? So I took my ruler and measure everything in sight. His command became my obsession. And I noticed I was measuring smaller and smaller objects.

WOLF: Why do you hide the figures under a carpet?

CYPRIAN: I don't hide them, that's where they want to go.

WOLF: Someone might tread on them. What are they made of? What raw materials do you use?

CYPRIAN: This one's made of earth. Soil combined with beeswax. And that one's jet. Polished coal. That's what they used to make amulets out of.

WOLF: Remarkable. Don't they remind you of those Minoan terracotta figures? The same primitive lust for life!

CYPRIAN: Don't know. Could be. Make something, he said, go on, make something. I'll give you the impulse, the eyes, the breath – and you get on with it. They're tiny little people, d'you see. Just sprites and hobgoblins, the sort that put holes in Catholics' condoms or itching powder in secretarys' knickers. (*Laughs.*) I used to make these enormous papier mâché things. Huge, bloody great things. So now he says, try something absolutely minute – see if it goes down any better.

WOLF: Who said this?

CYPRIAN: Oberon.

(*He produces another figure.*)

WOLF: It's fantastic.

CYPRIAN: She's called 'The curtsying schoolgirl'. She's got an injured knee. Been doing so many curtsies that the ligament's snapped. Now she's got a limp.

WOLF: The posture. The precision. Any moment you think she'd start scrabbling around in my hand.

CYPRIAN: (*Gives him a magnifying glass.*) Have a look, have a look.

WOLF: Her eyes. You can even see the expression in her eyes. You've made something extraordinary here.

CYPRIAN: Little devils, aren't they. Oh yes. So what d'you think. Will people like them?

WOLF: Why ask? Why should you care whether 'people' like them or not?

CYPRIAN: Sure. But still I'd like to know if they have any appeal. One tries to give pleasure and I often think – well, I'll give you a for-instance. When I'm working I like to listen to 'The Blue Danube' or 'Roses from the South', and I bet Johann, the Waltz King, thought, 'I wonder if people will go for this one? Oh yes, yes they're bound to like it. So *do* listen to it – it's for you. A gift from an artist.'

WOLF: The Waltz King, okay, fine. But you're a craftsman. What you make is silent, uncompromising – and only for a handful of cognoscenti.

CYPRIAN: Craftsman, eh? Is that all. Hardly seems worth the effort.

WOLF: No wait. I'd like to have this one. I'd like to buy it. 'The curtseying schoolgirl' with the wounded knee. I want to give it as a wedding present. A woman I'm in love with is marrying someone else.

CYPRIAN: I see. In that case don't take the girl. Take this one, here, horny little Titania, goddess of the moon. With her beside the bed, you can bet your little popsy will get all sorts of weird ideas about what makes a marriage.

WOLF: She's gorgeous. Lovelier than the others put together. What's she got in her hair, flowers?

CYPRIAN: Flowers? Ryvita, Carnation milk, marshmallows
and crisps. Titania is such a slut. She often walks amongst
men. In the supermarket, you know, during the day, when
it's not that busy. She just touches things and they follow
her of their own accord, and hover around her head like
planets. Which really pisses off the checkout girls, 'Why
can't you use a trolley like everyone else?' No, she's the
one you want, I promise. Her and no other.

WOLF: Yes, I'll take her.

CYPRIAN: (*Aside.*) Such a slut. She hurts me, torments me so
often… (*Aloud.*) So, you see. You've got to have ideas.
Sometimes you rack your brain for weeks, squeeze it like
a lemon. Nothing. And suddenly one day you give a little
cough – and Bob's your uncle!

SCENE 2

The park. TITANIA, the BLACK BOY sitting at her feet.

TITANIA: Out of this wood do not desire to go
Thou shalt remain here whether thou wilt or no
I am a spirit of no common rate,
The summer still doth tend upon my state;
And I do love thee: therefore go with me.
I'll give thee fairies to attend on thee:
And they shall fetch thee jewels from the deep
And sing whilst thou on pressed flowers dost sleep;
And I will purge thy mortal grossness so
That thou shalt like an airy spirit go.
Peaseblossom! Cobweb! Moth! and Mustardseed!
(*She pulls four white shirts out of the earth. Enter OBERON and
CYPRIAN who observe this scene from a distance.*)
Be kind and courteous to this gentleman
Hop in his walks and gambol in his eyes:
Feed him with apricocks and dewberries,
With purple grapes, green figs and mulberries;
The honey-bags steal from the humble-bees,
And for night-tapers crop their waxen thighs,
And light them at the fiery glow-worm's eyes,
To have my love to bed and to arise;

And pluck the wings from painted butterflies,
To fan the moonbeams from his sleeping eyes
Nod to him elves and do him courtesies.

OBERON: And there is sad Titania lost in dreams,
Now banished from her summer world, she acts
A sweet play for your blackamoor: the play
About the madwoman who married a donkey.

CYPRIAN: And this presumably is her farewell performance.

OBERON: And if she swore a thousand oaths to me
She'd still be running after anyone in trousers
And fraternizing almost randomly
But she can't help it, she can't stand this place,
The currents underground confuse her simple mind.

CYPRIAN: She pisses me off.

OBERON: Then show me how you can combine your art
With Oberon's spirit. Work a miracle. Find
The way to tame her wild majestic ways.
And banish her, shock treatment if you like,
For just a while, into a distant age.

(*Enter COURTLING, pushing an empty supermarket trolley.*)

TITANIA: Come wait on him: lead him to my bower
The moon methinks looks with a wat'ry eye.
And when she weeps, weeps every little flower,
Lamenting some enforced chastity…

(*She pushes the BLACK BOY away and runs to COURTLING.*)
Excuse me, can you tell me,
What the time is?

COURTLING: (*Who doesn't turn around.*) Yes. It's exactly…

TITANIA: It's you I've been waiting for, only you.
Every vista has been empty up to now,
I've stood on tiptoe, scanning it for you.

COURTLING: (*Amused and embarrassed.*) Ah, right…

TITANIA: Why will you not come into my fairy kingdom?
Across the park, past the fence, through rivers,
Through fire.

COURTLING: Well…

TITANIA: Where do you live?

COURTLING: Number Eight, Heimeranstrasse.

TITANIA: (*As if in a foreign language.*) What-have-you-got-in-the-deep freeze?

COURTLING: (*Seductively.*) In the deep freeze I have chicken pieces, pizza, Haagen-Dazs.

OBERON: Now!

CYPRIAN: (*To COURTLING.*) Her arms. Grab her arms.
(*She struggles but he succeeds in putting the amulet around her neck. She calms down, eventually stands still.*)

OBERON: (*To himself.*) Ah well. It works. And yet I feel this art
Will only serve to multiply my woes.

CYPRIAN: Thanks for helping out.

COURTLING: Don't mention it, Chip. But bloody hell, traumatic or what. I nearly had a heart attack!

SCENE 3

Wedding day. Podium, garlands. A column decked with flowers, TITANIA's statuette on it. HELEN in a wedding dress. GEORGE, WOLF, HELMA stand in a semi-circle behind the column. Even as they speak, they stare at the statuette.

HELEN: Oh God it's so cute.

GEORGE: Cute, well that's not exactly the word I'd…

HELEN: No I think it's real cute. Cute as anything. Real neat.
A sweet little darling. Such a refined little lady. What's her name?

HELMA: It's not a she.

GEORGE: It is.

WOLF: It's called 'Terror'.

HELEN: What?

GEORGE: Terra. As in 'terracotta'.

WOLF: No. Terror as in 'I'm terrified'. That which scares.

GEORGE: Oh great. The perfect wedding present.

WOLF: 'Terror. Titania the Tiger Cat.' That's what it's called.

HELEN: Look at her shining, sparkling.

WOLF: I was a little bit dubious at first, I'll admit it, 'cause of the rather ominous title. But it was far and away the most interesting piece in his studio. A real work of art, fully thought through.

HELMA: A work of art? That little doll? Not what I call art.

HELEN: Whatever, it's something to cherish. A good luck charm, a talisman.

WOLF: No, Helen, look I'm sorry; but it's a modern artwork. This artist is the pioneer of this new micro-miniature style. It cost me a good deal of money, actually.

GEORGE: It's *so* typical that these little things have become a craze overnight. I've even got a colleague who wears one round his neck in court, like an amulet.

WOLF: No, no. I think you're getting confused. Not a figurine like this one.

GEORGE: Excuse me. I'm not getting confused. It's absolutely *the* gift of the moment. 'The Thing', that's what they call it. Sort of half-jokingly but half not.

WOLF: Are you saying that my wedding present for Helen is some sort of kitsch tat from a cheap souvenir shop?

GEORGE: No of course I'm not saying that. I'm sure it was very expensive. But you see hundreds of these things all over the place now. They're all the rage.

HELMA: Talismen.

WOLF: Talismans, actually.

GEORGE: God, think of all the stupid crazes we've seen over the years. The Yo-Yo, the hula-hoop, the skateboard, the Sony Walkman, Rubik's cube. And now these little fertility gods are flooding the market. And I just think it's typical, that's all.

WOLF: Oh yes, typical of what?

GEORGE: Just typical. Everything that's effective nowadays, in science and technology, everything state of the art has to be tiny. Compact this and miniature that, everything is thumbnail sized. Small is beautiful, and small is getting smaller. Sign of the times. Micro-electronics, microfilm, and now, typically, micro-art.

WOLF: (*To HELEN.*) Do not believe a single word I beg you.
He's trying to poison you with utter nonsense.
Just look at her and feel the undertow.
A path of moonlight shimmers on the sea
And leads…

HELEN: (*To GEORGE.*) If I was to describe how I feel on this day
 I'd go all silly and old-fashioned and say,
 'I love you. I dote on you. I'm childishly,
 blindly crazy about you.'
GEORGE: Me too, about you. But beware, my love,
 That we don't wake up tomorrow morning like
 Two silly asses who don't even recognize one another.
HELEN: I have every confidence in my husband
 Who'll look after me if I should go astray.
HELMA: With any luck you'll be too shagged out to care!
GEORGE: Why don't you make yourself a bit more
 comfortable, change out of your wedding dress before the
 party?
HELEN: I'm gonna run around in my dream dress,
 'Til it gets as dirty and black and stiff as
 Some nigger bastard.
HELMA: Oh no – that's done it.
WOLF: (*To HELEN.*) I'm sorry…
HELMA: What about?
WOLF: I'm sorry, Helen…
HELMA: What about?
WOLF: (*Screams at her.*) You shut up!
 I'm sorry if I caused you undue distress
 Or if its title, 'Terror', has disturbed you.
 It wasn't my intention to upset you.
HELEN: But I love it, I love it.

SCENE 4

Park. TITANIA – transformed into 'The Woman from Another Age'. A tight outdoor costume, crinoline. She looks stiff and frightened as the THREE BOYS and the FIRST GIRL surround her.

FIRST BOY: What sort of zoo did you break out of then? You're
 really pretty, you are.
SECOND BOY: She's out the museum. Out the gallery.
THIRD BOY: What, can't you speak? Where did you come
 from? Not from round here?

(*TITANIA makes her seemingly reflex action of opening her coat, if she had one, to expose herself.*)

SECOND BOY: What's yer name?

FIRST GIRL: She don't understand.

FIRST BOY: Bet she can't even hear us.

THIRD BOY: What's your name!!

FIRST BOY: (*Shouts.*) Can-you-hear-me?

FIRST GIRL: She's not from now, this day and age.

THIRD BOY: What d'you mean?

FIRST BOY: All right, if she's from a different day and age

Then she'd better fucking tell us

What it was like, before…

THIRD BOY: (*Snaps his fingers in TITANIA's face.*)

Go on tell us.

SECOND BOY: Says nothing, hears nothing, sees nothing.

FIRST GIRL: (*Presses her toy dog into TITANIA's hands.*)

She can't even hold the dog.

She can't hang on to anything.

THIRD BOY: (*Stuffs his headphones into her mouth.*) Perhaps she can taste.

FIRST BOY: (*Throws an empty beer can at her head.*)

Perhaps she can think.

SECOND BOY: Hey you, woman in a time-warp!

THIRD BOY: (*Rips his headphones out of her mouth.*)

Don't you fucking break my things.

Cow! (*Goes nearer.*)

FIRST GIRL: (*Singing out loud.*) There's a lot of people in the park.

ALL THREE BOYS: (*In chorus.*) Yeah, lots of people walking about.

(*ALL FOUR dance around TITANIA, singing.*)

THIRD BOY: Where d'you come from then? Antiques Roadshow?

FIRST GIRL: Older than that.

THIRD BOY: Blast from the past.

FIRST GIRL: No, older!

THIRD BOY: Relic from the mummy's tomb!

FIRST GIRL: No, miles older!

THIRD BOY: Prehistoric monster!

FIRST BOY: You've got a face haven't you

You're not made of plastic

Open your gob then, go on.

(*The FIRST BOY goes up to her, still dancing. She pushes her flat hand into his face. ALL FOUR fall onto their backs.*)

THIRD BOY: That came from up there.

FIRST BOY: Fuck. Let's go.

(*The BOYS run away. The FIRST GIRL with her dog stays, squatting on the ground.*)

FIRST GIRL: I haven't been here very long.

I don't yet know what I'm doing here.

It feels all right though, sort of.

I walk around the streets a lot

But I don't know the houses from inside

Sometimes I think, everyone else is okay

It's just me spends all my time

On the outside looking in.

And I feel so much of my own strength

Turned inwards, against myself.

I don't know why.

My old man's had enough – my mum

Spends all day bawling her eyes out

So I slashed his tyres the other day.

I'll do waitressing if I have to.

I'll keep working until it all

Starts going wrong again.

(*TITANIA slowly lowers her hand onto the FIRST GIRL's hair. When she touches her, the FIRST GIRL's face seems suddenly racked with pain.*)

SCENE 5

WOLF and HELMA's place. WOLF lies on the ground, his head buried in a map. HELMA looks out into the park. Night. Sounds of a zoo; crickets.

HELMA: Once you used to tell me about the constellations.

You knew where Sirius was in Canis Major,

And all the facts about it. But nowadays,

You've forgotten everything. And I bet

You don't gaze at the sky at night at all.

Your silence speaks volumes, as usual.

We live on the sunny side of the park.

It only takes a couple of minutes' walk
And we could be beside that little stream.
The one you used to love so much –
When did you last go down there? Eh? Not for months
For months, you've been spending all your free time
Lying on your belly, looking at your maps
And moping about.
Wolf! We can't just look out at the park like it's something
that doesn't concern us. We have to go in! We have to
go back in together! Come on, you daft old thing! You
used to be able to tell me the whole story of the French
Revolution, painting such wonderful pictures with your
words. Today I bet you wouldn't even know when it took
place. Or if it ever even did. I mean there's such a wealth
of knowledge going to waste. We're both from good
families, well brought up. How can it have come to this,
not knowing the basic facts of world history or the universe
any more. I bet you'd fail your A-levels if you took them
now! There's remedial students more clued up than you
are now.

WOLF: There's absolutely no reason for me to remember
about the French Revolution.

HELMA: 'Cause now you hate it. Like you hate everything,
nowadays. Even the stars. Which is why, effectively you
don't understand anything any more.

WOLF: The stars are too much for anyone to understand.

HELMA: And before? In history? How about early man, he got
his mind round them somehow. Inventing legends, fairy
tales, anything to stop the universe from dropping on his head.

WOLF: What day is it today?

HELMA: Tuesday. Wednesday.

WOLF: (*Leaps to his feet.*) Tuesdaywednesday!

HELMA: Tuesday – or Wednesday.

WOLF: Well, which? Don't leave me guessing.

HELMA: I'm not that sure myself.

WOLF: You see if it's that hard to get to grips with something
as immediate as which day of the week it is – it doesn't
encourage me to discuss something as remote as the
French Revolution.

HELMA: There was a time when you brought the French Revolution so close to me, that it could have happened yesterday.

WOLF: I'm afraid one is totally misrepresenting the French Revolution if one pretends it happened yesterday. It didn't happen yesterday, that's the point actually.

HELMA: So, when *did* it happen? When was it?

(*WOLF remains silent.*)

Oh yes, it was 'way back when', wasn't it? 'Way back when.' Isn't that what you normally say nowadays?

WOLF: Normally say? Since when have I 'normally said' that?

HELMA: Since way back when!

WOLF: Be precise, when?

HELMA: Since you stopped knowing things.

Since we stopped reading.

Since we stopped travelling.

Since we stopped being what we were.

WOLF: You're not being precise.

HELMA: Okay. Since that time you got Danton and Robespierre mixed up.

WOLF: Aha. So you remember that do you? That's probably all you do remember about the French Revolution.

HELMA: But how could I forget? When that little slip marked the end of any further tales of the French Revolution.

WOLF: Mixing up Robespierre with Danton is unfortunately rather more than just a little slip.

HELMA: For God's sake. So tell about them! Tell me their story. Tell me everything there is to know about them. Go on.

WOLF: I mixed them up.

HELMA: Yes and that's all, that's absolutely all you now know about, about that – pair of…prats!

SCENE 6

All-night café in the park. All the characters, save TITANIA, are sitting alone, or severally at tables, relaxing. FIRSTLING and COURTLING, the advertising salesman and the out-of-work architect, are deep in conversation.

COURTLING: It starts in the bridge of my nose and then goes upwards. I'm telling you I haven't been taking anything for it. But I've got this terrible headache and I can't roll my eyes any more. I haven't had a headache like this – not for years.

FIRSTLING: (*Overly concerned.*) Okay. Symptoms. What are your symptoms?

COURTLING: Look at this. The skin's hanging down over this eye. (*FIRSTLING gets up, casts an expert eye over the problem.*) My whole face is tensed up, it could tear in half. There's a beating in my ears. And a pressure on my brain.

FIRSTLING: So what's your diagnosis? Your facial muscles are…it's like your face is sort of hanging off?

COURTLING: My diagnosis…

FIRSTLING: So you have one?

COURTLING: I do. It's, well, like the thing I had before with my arms.

FIRSTLING: You had a thing?

COURTLING: With my arms, yes, it was unbearable. I was screaming with pain. I was saying, go on, amputate my arms, both of them, I can't bear it! I was in the Stiermayer clinic. A mistake as it turned out! They just give you injections, almost at random, you could be at the vet's. Can't you give me the address of a good doctor?

FIRSTLING: Who were you with when you had the arm thing?

COURTLING: If it's the same thing now that I had in my arms, and I strongly suspect it is, then forget it. I couldn't go through that again.

FIRSTLING: Have you been abroad?

COURTLING: Abroad? No, no, it's nothing like that.

FIRSTLING: (*Behind his hand.*) Infections!

COURTLING: Come on, *politicians* travel abroad the whole time.

FIRSTLING: Yes, they do. But they're much better looked after than you are. (*Jumps up, goes to his coat.*) I think I've got just the thing for you. (*He produces a piece of dental equipment.*) There. Someone brought it into the agency this morning. Do-It-Yourself Dentist's Kit. Not yet available on the open market. Not in Germany. DIY dentistry. No adapter, no battery, you just plug it into the mains. No, it's brilliant, you could unblock your own urethra with that thing. (*Turns round.*) Whoops, I'll keep my voice down... There we go. You've gone and broken it. Didn't last long.

COURTLING: Come off it. It's just one of those new toothbrushes. That's all.

FIRSTLING: Unavailable on the open market.

COURTLING: What are you going on about? It's just one of those toothbrushes, just like the other ones, you know, electric ones. Just a bit more powerful.

FIRSTLING: That's that. You've broken it. Won't go anymore. Totally unavailable. (*Notices an insect by the flower vase.*) Oh look. A frog-hopper. It's an insect – doesn't fly, just hops. Just like my mother says, you've got to travel light to keep on the move.

COURTLING: You're still buying those expensive shirts.

FIRSTLING: What? This shirt? My dear chap, it's ten years old. Ten years old.

COURTLING: And what's that? You've always got something new.

FIRSTLING: An amulet. No, stop it. Get your hands off.

FIRSTLING: Everyone wants out of Germany. Soon there'll be no one left but me and the Chancellor.

COURTLING: Only the captain and the rat stay on board.

FIRSTLING: Oh, the rat! Well, I'm not the rat, I assure you. But it's all going to get worse, you know. The recession.

COURTLING: The boss of TWA...

FIRSTLING: Continental: losing a billion dollars every –

COURTLING: TWA's a much bigger outfit. In Chicago or somewhere this boss sends his secretary out, to get coffee or something. Then bang, he's blown his brains out. Bang, bang...splash.

FIRSTLING: You must have read that in the *Frankfurter Allgemeine* didn't you?

COURTLING: No actually it was *Newsweek.*

FIRSTLING: Then they must have printed the Frankfurt piece.

COURTLING: Well at least I haven't got a BMW fixation like you have.

FIRSTLING: Now you've got Porsche-mania.

COURTLING: Well you've got – you've got...

FIRSTLING: Oh stop it.

COURTLING: No, you stop it. You've always been in a different tax bracket from me. You'd never be seen dead in anything less than a BMW.

FIRSTLING: Pigs might fly. My God, time certainly does, doesn't it? On the twenty-second we were burying poor old Heinnard. That was three days ago.

COURTLING: Is it the twenty-fifth?

FIRSTLING: (*Checking his watch.*) The twenty-sixth. God, I was just thinking, three years, that's thirty-six months.

COURTLING: What, you're paying by instalments?

FIRSTLING: Thirty-six months, that's one hundred and forty-four weeks.

COURTLING: What, weekly instalments?

FIRSTLING: It's dog eat dog.

(*COURTLING takes his glasses off.*)

You ought to clean your glasses. Soak them in saline solution.

COURTLING: It's just here, on the bridge of my nose. There could be a thousand explanations. Even hereditary ones.

FIRSTLING: So where did you go when you had that thing with your arms?

COURTLING: To the Stiermayer clinic.

FIRSTLING: Hey, listen. I know an excellent orthopaedist.

COURTLING: An orthopaedist?

FIRSTLING: Yes. You don't believe me?

COURTLING: What's my face got to do with an orthopaedist? I need a neurologist!

FIRSTLING: Fine, suit yourself.

COURTLING: Oh, who cares anyway?

The whole country's going to the dogs.

And it's nothing to do with us.

Or rather everything to do with us!

I give it two more years, or three, at most.

Blackout.

Act Three

SCENE 1

GEORGE and HELEN's place.

GEORGE: Why were you being so abusive to that black kid?

HELEN: Which one do you mean?

GEORGE: Just now in the bus.

HELEN: Oh, I just can't stand niggers, that's all.

GEORGE: But he wasn't bothering you.

HELEN: Not bothering me? That stinking pig, that nigger pawing my knee the whole time. 'Oh my you're looking real pretty li'l lady. Wanna see some hot pictures? Take a look at my…' That creep was all over me.

GEORGE: Just this kid, showing off a bit, okay very aware of his own body; the bus was swaying to and fro, okay, maybe he went a bit far.

HELEN: 'Keep your dirty fingers off me and beat it. You nigger son of a bitch. Stop touching me!'

GEORGE: But God, you know, that really takes some nerve – to dare to be so openly insulting to a young black guy. I'm amazed he took it so well.

HELEN: (*Whimpers theatrically.*) 'Hey, that lady there pushed me – that lady say I touch her. But I didn't never lay a finger on her – no siree.'

GEORGE: When he got off he stuck his tongue out at you like a little kid.

HELEN: These niggerboys should learn to behave like the other decent, ordinary passengers. If we're going to have to share a bus with them.

GEORGE: What's got into you?

HELEN: Nothing. Niggers are inferior, that's all.

GEORGE: You don't really believe that yourself, surely.

HELEN: You bet I do. It's been proved – they're more devious, more lazy, more prone to violence than other people.

GEORGE: That's complete nonsense.

HELEN: It's not nonsense. I've lived around niggers. I know what I'm talking about.

GEORGE: Helen! You're a reasonable woman. You can't, not now not ever, turn round and say that black people are second-class citizens.

HELEN: I've got nothing against blacks. Just niggers. Chinks are fine – they're tough people, undemanding. They work all the hours God sends.

GEORGE: No, no. Please. That's enough.

HELEN: Okay, I'm not going to bother to fight for my convictions. But I'm not going to renounce them either.

GEORGE: You're on edge today, baby. It's 'cause Wolf's coming, right? Ah well, I'm off soon. I normally organise it so that you see each other when I'm in the office. You'll spend another pleasant afternoon together. We've been getting on so well lately, Wolf and I. So much harmony between your two favourite men. You seem to get quite misty-eyed when you see us together. You don't mind me calling us 'your two favourite men', do you?

HELEN: Why should I? You know anyway.

GEORGE: I know nothing. (*He stands up.*) Right, then…

HELEN: George?

GEORGE: Yup?

HELEN: We're okay aren't we? I mean, we've got no reason to worry, have we? I mean about money?

GEORGE: No. Why do you ask?

HELEN: I keep on hearing people grumbling about the way things are going, worrying about the future.

GEORGE: We don't need to, but –

HELMA: 'Cause I don't want to wake up one morning
And find the crisis has got to us too.
So please be even more careful than before.
I get this feeling we should be aiming for something,
Some really sensational success. Some breakthrough.
Don't you agree? Have you got anything lined up?
Are you defending well? Are you sure you're not
Losing too many cases?
Are you taking on clients with the money to pay?
Are the amounts involved worth the effort?

GEORGE: But sweetheart, why are you worrying like this?

HELEN: I've got this real longing for success.

This animal longing – for success.

GEORGE: You should go back to work yourself.

HELEN: No: you must work. I want you strong

And smart, the top of the heap. I want

To feel all your strength, every ounce of it. So

You've gotta work hard, so damn hard.

No setbacks, no reverses, no dithering.

You see, I demand a lot of you. I want

A man who always wins. And as he wins

Gets stronger, stronger, stronger every day.

Who takes me, conquers me, and makes me happy.

Who'll love me forever. And loads of money, George,

Money for the kids, their education, money for us.

Money for our old age, money for beauty.

Money.

(*GEORGE goes to her. She raises her arm to protect her face, as if
she was expecting to be hit. But he comes to embrace her.*)

(*Laughing.*) Over the chair, over the chair.

(*CYPRIAN is suddenly in the room.*)

CYPRIAN: What are you doing? Are you mad? I lost an ear in
the war. The monkeys are all dead. The grass is all dead.
And serve you right. Nowadays we all have to register.
You're not allowed to build any more roads. You have to
register with the Civil Defence. Take your hands off me.
Get your hands off!

GEORGE: Who are you? What do you want?

CYPRIAN: You! You've been lodging with Mother Nature.
And you've been standing at the railway station. I saw you
in the cinema. Don't walk so fast. I was wounded in the
war, me too! It's all on computer – they have to tell you
nowadays. Oh yes. So stop it, now, okay! That's enough!
Whatever happened to planning permission?

HELEN: (*Whispering.*) Help, help.

CYPRIAN: (*Laughs.*) No, no. Fooled you. Just a joke. I appear to
have lost my way.

GEORGE: For God's sake. Get the fuck out of my house.

CYPRIAN: These modern open-plan eco-houses, you don't
know what's public and what's private. No doors, you see.

GEORGE: (*To HELEN.*) You've forgotten to shut the gate properly again. (*Leading CYPRIAN upstage.*) Come along, this way...

CYPRIAN: The ancient Chinese knew that the whole earth was criss-crossed with magic paths. Ley-lines, if you like. And there's definitely one running through your sitting-room. I'd have it looked into if I was you.

GEORGE: (*Returns.*) The park is full of nutters wandering about. And if you don't shut the door properly they'll get into the house.

HELEN: Yes, George.

GEORGE: What I wanted to say earlier was; you know your attack on... You surely weren't serious were you?

HELEN: Not serious? Why should I pretend?

GEORGE: But where do you get so much hate from?

HELEN: Who knows. From my head. But it's in my blood too.

GEORGE: Has a black ever done you any harm?

HELEN: They're repulsive. Isn't that enough? They're evil incarnate. They're out to get the white race and crush them, stifle them, trample all over them.

GEORGE: I thought you said they were lazy.

HELEN: Lazy and power-hungry.

GEORGE: I'm a lawyer, Helen. Professionally I have to stand up for the rights of the weak, the oppressed, the minorities.

HELEN: Yeah. Fine. Great. I respect that. But what's that gotta do with niggers? We haven't got any negroes round here, we don't come into contact with them. So why fall out over it? It's like one half of a couple is Protestant, the other half Catholic. They can each hang on to their respective beliefs and still have a good marriage.

GEORGE: But it's not possible that I'm married to a self-confessed racist.

HELEN: Oh yes it is!

GEORGE: My God, what a dirty trick. Why didn't you tell me this before. You shouldn't be allowed out, spreading your sick opinions. I should have been told at the outset!

SCENE 2

Entrance to a house on the park. Moonlight. TITANIA, dressed as 'The Woman from Another Age', walks slowly, as if drawn from a distance towards the house. We can hear her dress rustling. COURTLING leaves his house. Dark suit, cap, glasses, rolled-up umbrella. Carefully, he locks the door. By now TITANIA is behind him. He says hallo and walks on. TITANIA turns the handle, enters his house. He turns round, notices his door is open, shakes his head, goes back, examines the lock, locks the door again, sets off. Suddenly he stops and says, 'What do you want in my house?' Runs back, unlocks the door, enters. Shortly after, a long scream, starting in a man's voice, ending in a child's. TITANIA appears at the door, a ten year-old boy in her arms. A miniature replica of COURTLING, identically clad. She takes the little man to the sand-pit, and sets him down so he can look into the brightly lit opening of the circus curtain. She disappears behind the hedge.

SCENE 3

FIRSTLING and the FIRST GIRL with her toy dog.

FIRSTLING: You're probably not as robust as the others.
You've got very delicate shoulder-blades.

FIRST GIRL: Shoulder-blades in humans are actually vestigial wings.

FIRSTLING: You don't say.

FIRST GIRL: It's true.

(She takes a salt-cellar out of her jeans' pocket, and sprinkles salt into her mouth.)

The others are okay, they're more grown up. It's just me who's on the outside looking in the whole time.

FIRSTLING: *(Nervously.)* Aha…

FIRST GIRL: I haven't been here very long. I don't yet know what I'm doing here. It feels all right, though: sort of.

FIRSTLING: Hm, hm. I have high hopes, you know, of finding some real human warmth against this backdrop of general disorder. Vandalism, desperation, burning boxes, burning tyres…

FIRST GIRL: I feel so much of my own strength turned inwards against myself.

FIRSTLING: Hm, well, there we go…

FIRST GIRL: (*Putting more salt in her mouth.*) I can eat salt by the spoonful.

FIRSTLING: Ah, good. Though sooner or later you'll be kissing someone's mouth… (*Giggles.*)

FIRST GIRL: Here's what I see. The great big world of technology on one side and the tiny stinky world of the poor pigs on the other.

FIRSTLING: Hm, hm. But you can't deny we have made some progress. Public Health, for example. That can't be cancelled out overnight.

FIRST GIRL: Public Health. That's the pits. Just makes things worse – that's what gives you fungus and zits and all the other crap you get on your skin.

FIRSTLING: Hm, hm.

(*They have arrived at the hedge. FIRSTLING casts anxious glances to all sides of the stage.*)

FIRST GIRL: I had this dream again last night. All families had been got rid of. Like they've been disappeared. So you're just sort of born somewhere and slotted into society straight away. So you don't feel you've ever had a family or nothing. Just a few vague circles of friends, people from work, from school, people where you live, and all that.

FIRSTLING: A nightmare.

FIRST GIRL: Not really. There's a lot of truth in it.

FIRSTLING: Oh, you haven't got any relatives, then?

FIRST GIRL: Me? Sure. Yeah.

(*As she puts the salt-cellar in her mouth again, FIRSTLING drags her underneath the hedge.*)

FIRSTLING: Come here, you dirty little Mickey Mouse. I'll make you the most beautiful woman in Europe. If you'd only keep still. I'll give you such sparkle, such elegance. Your wish is my command. But if you start taking the piss, like Betty Peters, then I'll beat you to a pulp. You're my proud princess now. You have to be proud, so proud, then it'll be all fine, then –

(*He gives a cry of pain. GIRL emerges from under the hedge. Gathers her glasses, her dog, brushes earth off her clothes.*)

FIRST GIRL: Dickhead!

(*The THREE BOYS come with a net made of ropes.*)

FIRST BOY: Grab hold of it. We're gonna catch the woman from long ago.

THIRD BOY: Come on, come with us. We're gonna catch Godzilla and sell her to the museum.

FIRST GIRL: Nah. Don't wanna.

THIRD BOY: She sent him a letter.

SECOND BOY: Out the sky. It was hanging out the sky, between two clouds. This fucking great big letter. Then it fell in the field. I ran through the park. Tried to read it. But I was too near, the letters were too big. So I climbed a tree, read it from up there –

THIRD BOY: Yeah and d'you know what it said? She wants to meet him. Nico! On his own... But we're all going. Now we'll catch the beast...

FIRST GIRL: You're making it up. Fuck off.

(*The BOYS run off left. The GIRL exits right. FIRSTLING sticks his head out of the hedge, looks about. Mumbles something like 'Nothing's as good as it's cracked up to be', crawls out, rearranges his clothes.*)

FIRSTLING: (*To himself.*) *Je suis comme je suis.* It makes you wonder; what's an upright decent person doing, getting himself into such ludicrous contortions, just for a bit of fun? These were the ingredients: half-hearted desire, suspicion, sexual intercourse. After that it all got a bit like Betty Peters... No, that's not fair. She was charming. Why so critical after the event? Why pick retrospective holes in a coupling which was in itself perfectly rounded, perfectly whole? Talk about deconstruction! You're hardly back on your feet and your head's crawling with words. Just then it was the physical reality of a bit of flat ground, a few silent, rapid, joyous thrusts – and now, afterwards, abstract thoughts, abstract violence. But what's making me have these thoughts, her behaviour, that's what...

(*He moves back. COURTLING by the sand-pit makes a little noise. 'Ee!' FIRSTLING stops, listens, then goes up to the little man.*)

Hallo, little chap. Isn't it past your bedtime? You're terribly smart. You going out tonight?

(*The little man makes a little noise. 'Ee!'*)

Now what's the matter? Let's have a look at you! Good heavens, Courtling! What's happened? For God's sake, can you hear me? Oh God, the symptoms, the symptoms – what are your symptoms? It's the end – it's come. It's got you, Courtling. Come along, I'll bring you to nice Mr Doctor. Christ Almighty, what have you been doing? Now don't cry, little boy, I'm right here. I'll help you, don't you worry. You're still in one piece. Come on, old boy, I'll take you to my orthopaedist… Oh bollocks, that's no good, is it? We'll have to go somewhere else. But where?

(*He takes COURTLING by the hand, exits behind the hedge.*)

SCENE 4

Enter GEORGE and WOLF.

WOLF: No. George, I think you're being a bit harsh. You must look deep into her face. You'll see that Helen is something very special.

GEORGE: Very special! Well she's turned into a very special pain in the arse. What bugs me is that she's so weird. That pretty head of hers, it's worm-eaten. From the outside it's so fresh and gorgeous but inside it's maggot-ridden. And she's poisoning me with her pestilent opinions.

WOLF: Now you're just being critical. You should be helping her, giving her peace and quiet and love. It's just her childhood tears. You're taking it far too seriously.

GEORGE: She's slipping away from me, regressing. Every day I feel more distant, she notices me less and less. And then, recently, I feel it taking me over, like demonic possession, and I'm sharing her obscene beliefs. What thing have I married? My own stupidity gave me the go-ahead and led me to this evil witch. My own bloody stupidity!

WOLF: I don't see it like that at all. Okay I agree she's strange, but strange like wonderful, rare, precious – like a jewel.

GEORGE: (*Hanging onto WOLF.*) I've got to mix with better people. Show me some better people, Wolf. I've had enough of talking to these ghouls. I'd rather spend my time with trolls or fairies than with productivity experts and high tax-bracket bloody piss-artists. I'd rather be a blowfly on a dung heap than be surrounded by psychologists and magistrates and social workers. I'd rather be a tapeworm in their shit than to have to meet them face to face. I'd rather be a godlin in my Grandma's bottling jar than a state subsidised self-realiser in his open-plan cage, surrounded by crap and fetid heat and baby monkeys with dead eyes, little puppies already sick of life. I don't get on with anyone any more. I sit in the pub every evening and slag off all my friends. Oh God, where did it come from, this total despair? I don't normally see things in such a cold and glaring light. Wolf, we're going to have to stick so close together from now on, do you see? You're the only one I can really trust!

WOLF: What about Helen?

GEORGE: Helen, Helen. The only thing about me you're interested in. I no sooner give you a hug than you're sniffing round my clothes to catch a whiff of her.

WOLF: If you're going to be tasteless you can do your grizzling on your own.

GEORGE: Wolf, no stay with me. Guess what I've done? I've started up a marketing company. This advertising guy, this unemployed architect and me.

WOLF: What are you marketing?

GEORGE: We're producing short films about holidays. To save the rainforest, instead of expensive glossy brochures, you'll be able to go to the travel agent or whatever and get one of our tapes. You say 'Elba', and then you get to see what it's like. What the fuck am I doing with my life?

WOLF: You probably want to make some decent money for a change.

GEORGE: Are you sure we're awake? Sometimes I feel that we're asleep and it's something else that's awake... And the fact that no one, no one wakes us up is because we're so consumed by sleep that there is no waking up as such, just continual change, continual metamorphosis. And walking alongside are the ghosts, the dead and the undead, and they influence us all the time. So the dead and the living are all mixed together, all equal. Our skulls are as thin as eggshell, Wolf, that's why the ancient shadows are starting to seep in. God, I'm so stupid. What have I married?

WOLF: Look, it's fine. You set up a new business, and of course you feel the earth is crumbling beneath your feet. And that you're being sucked under.

SCENE 5

CYPRIAN and HELMA meet in the park.

HELMA: Chip!

CYPRIAN: At last. There you are. I've been looking for you everywhere. I've even been walking into other people's houses.

HELMA: Did you bring the figurine?

CYPRIAN: Hang on, hang on. Why didn't you come to my studio? (*He unwraps his handkerchief to reveal a tiny medallion.*)

HELMA: Let me see. What is it?

CYPRIAN: Can't you see? It's a woman immured up to the neck. She's sticking her neck out and crying for help. So she's a bawling brat. White wall, bawling brat, and that's that.

HELMA: And is it supposed to work?

CYPRIAN: Yes. It'll work.

HELMA: God it's so ugly.

CYPRIAN: Give it me back.

HELMA: No. I'm sure it's a real work of art. I just don't understand these things. I need it, though, I need it. Here, take the money, Chip… How do you make them so expressive? And you wear it round your neck?

CYPRIAN: Yes. Or lower down.

HELMA: And then what happens?

CYPRIAN: It summons people. As many as you want. Men. As many as you can handle! You can take your pick.

HELMA: I only want one. Mine.

CYPRIAN: Yes, he'll come too. You've got the original there. Most people only get factory copies.

HELMA: These little things have caught on world-wide. A real epidemic, eh?

CYPRIAN: Have you got kids?

HELMA: No. Unfortunately not.

CYPRIAN: Well now you've got a Bawling Brat. (*They laugh.*) A baby at your breast, it doesn't make a sound, but it's still a Bawling Brat. What is it?… Yup. Today we're having a laugh together. But tomorrow you'll smash my head in with a fencepost with a four-inch nail stuck in it.

HELMA: Who will?

CYPRIAN: You will. Or people like you.

HELMA: You're mad, do you hear? Sick! Mad!

(*She runs off.*)

SCENE 6

The bushes. TITANIA under a net, which is hammered into the ground like a tent. The THREE BOYS and the FIRST GIRL, thus: SECOND BOY next to the GIRL; further off, FIRST BOY next to THIRD BOY.

FIRST BOY: (*To THIRD BOY.*) You cold? Have my pullover.

SECOND BOY: (*To GIRL.*) You gotta be honest. Every morning you gotta find the rotten bits, get rid of them, spit them out.

FIRST GIRL: Not that easy.

FIRST BOY: (*To THIRD BOY.*) Are you okay? I'll stand guard for you if you like.

SECOND BOY: Only if you're honest. That's the only way you'll make it. No cheating. You gotta see yourself like clear water – crystal clear, ice cold. That's basically what you gotta be like if you're gonna accept yourself. Totally.

FIRST GIRL: That's right. Then you can go to Tibet and get a stone and chuck it down, from the roof of the world and listen to it rolling down, not stopping, just rolling down and down.

FIRST BOY: (*To THIRD BOY.*) You like 'Empty Love' by the Migs? I'll copy it for you.

SECOND BOY: For instance. Human sexuality.

FIRST GIRL: Oh fuck, don't start that again.

SECOND BOY: No, honest. You ought to stop being on the lookout. I mean Prince Charming isn't always gonna come along, is he?

FIRST GIRL: No, but I've made my decision. If I say to myself, Okay you're on your own, out in the rain, then you don't have to worry about it, 'cause it's boring and you know you're not gonna bump into anything weird and wonderful.

SECOND BOY: Yeah, except you bumped into me and I'm pretty weird and wonderful.

THIRD BOY: I'd like to row a boat through Ireland.

FIRST BOY: If that's what you want – then we'll do it.

THIRD BOY: We got no money to hire a boat.

FIRST BOY: P'raps we could find a broken one and do it up.

FIRST GIRL: I could just as well have reached a different decision. I could've said, 'Okay, I'll get married.' Like my sister. Or someone. You always hope. Everyone hopes. That's only normal.

SCENE 7

WOLF and HELMA's flat. Terrace. Two chairs. HELMA, dressed only in a shirt, leans against the doorway and smokes.

WOLF: How's Helen been?

GEORGE: Fine. She's fine. Abso-bloody-lutely fine. She's been completely taken over by political coprolalia.

WOLF: What's that?

GEORGE: It's a morbid compulsion to be endlessly spouting reactionary crap. You meet this gorgeous girl. Turns out she's branch secretary of the local Ku Klux Klan.

WOLF: She'll claw her way back, you'll see.

(He goes into the flat with an empty bottle.)

GEORGE: *(To HELMA.)* You're running around with practically nothing on.

HELMA: It's hot.

GEORGE: Sit down here.

(He puts his clenched fist, with the thumb sticking out, on the chair.
HELMA sits slowly.)

HELMA: (*Without even looking.*) And you can take your filthy
  paw away for a start.

GEORGE: Oh yes, naked are we? Dead trendy, very now.
  (*HELMA smokes.*)
  And? Sweating, shaking, squealing, everything okay, is it?

HELMA: Everything's fine.
  (*WOLF comes back. HELMA goes up to him. He puts his right*
  hand on her cheek, his left hand on her hip. She snuggles her face
  up to WOLF's hand, looking at him. Suddenly she snaps at his
  hand, holds it in her teeth, like a dog might a bird.)

GEORGE: It's midsummer night.
  Shipwrecks turn on ocean beds.
  Horses can speak.
  Loving couples leap through bonfires
  And sick women roll in the morning dew.

SCENE 8

The bushes. Music. Roaring of a bull. FIRST BOY sleeps, down from
TITANIA. The circus curtain billows forward covering the captured
TITANIA. Bull's horns poke through the curtain. When the curtain retreats,
TITANIA is free, her costume torn to shreds.

SCENE 9

HELEN and WOLF walk into the park.

HELEN: (*Points to the ground.*) What's that?

WOLF: Oh, surprisingly enough, it's just a spot of something.
  Cuckoo-spit? A spot anyway, from the manifold panoply
  of nature.

HELEN: From a hanged man!

WOLF: There are no gallows round here.
  Not even a tree. The empty sky,
  You'd be hard pressed to hang yourself on that.

HELEN: The spot comes from a hanged man!
  Which makes it doubly cursed.

For such a spot could grow into a hundred
Mandrake roots.
And they're the gallows-men. They can raise
The birth rate in this area from five-fold
To eight-fold.

WOLF: You're completely seized up with superstition. It's no
more than a moist bit of cuckoo-spit.

HELEN: Cuckoo-spit. Ha, and what do you think that is?
Something a cuckoo spits out of a tree?

WOLF: How should I know? Some form of excretion from the
cuckoo, yes.

HELEN: Gotcha. That's crap. Cuckoo-spit is the protective
froth of the grasshopper larva. It produces this waxy
secretion which it combines with its own liquid shit and
froths the whole lot up with air.

WOLF: Is that true, or more of your gobbledygook? I've always
assumed that stuff was, well, as the name suggests –

HELEN: You see, clever-clogs, car-owner, it comes to
something when a person who still thinks like a nine year-
old accuses someone else of superstition. You're talking out
of your ass!

SCENE 10

TITANIA in CYPRIAN's studio.

TITANIA: Daedalus. Can you make cows too?

CYPRIAN: What are you after? I didn't call you. Clear off. Do
some work. Stop frightening me.

TITANIA: Longing, such longing. Are you listening?

CYPRIAN: I've nothing to say to you. I'm working on
something new.

TITANIA: I'm floating on, protected by
This mad sea of sensations. His misty
Breath still hangs around me, like some madness.
If and when I come to my senses – my heart
Will not survive the shock.
Daedalus – I've gone mad. For a bull.

CYPRIAN: What did you call me? Who're you being now?
Titania of the moon, beware. You like to

56

Appear in so many guises, that sometimes you
Get them muddled up.
It isn't right to have so many shapes.
Consider the serious consequences of
Your Majesty's behaviour. You can't make the rules up
As you go along.

TITANIA: Don't try and teach me what I know too well.
Are you not Daedalus, Statue-maker?

CYPRIAN: I am Cyprian. You know, Chip.

TITANIA: Come on, come on, do not dissemble. I am Pasiphae
and you are Daedalus, the man who entertains my
husband King Minos and all our little children with your
puppets. Your living dolls and other playthings. Once you
sent an ant with a thread into a seashell. A tiny Ariadne in
a labyrinth. And now you must help me. I am screaming
and every part of me screams too, with longing for that
great white beast. I'm bursting for him, burning. My vulva
is bloated like a cow's. The pink, the shiny skin all swollen
with thick dark lips and viscous slime. Not like a woman's
wetness, more like cow's. My muzzle's hot and fetid – cow
again. Pains and more pains. Not just throbbing blood but
endless, deep and endless trembling, longing to be taken
– make me a cow's arse! I cannot bear it, for he'll never
come and take me as I am, too small for him, too human to
excite him.

CYPRIAN: Perhaps you've forgotten. But I am mad for
somebody as well. Someone wonderful. Who won't give
me a second glance.

TITANIA: You can never understand my need. The human race
knows nothing of desire.

CYPRIAN: Now you know exactly how I feel. When I am
longing for my Black Boy.

TITANIA: Make me an extension. Thick and round, and soft
as moss – but not too fat. My beloved's flanks are white as
snow. He wears a coronet of hyacinths around his neck.
His brow is cold as marble. Daedalus – I'm ashamed to
be like this. Stuck here in this narrow woman's body. A
half-cadaverous thing like me will never tempt the God of
Beasts.

CYPRIAN: I used to work quite a lot in larger forms...

TITANIA: A cow, damn you! A hollow cow!

CYPRIAN: No, no. I serve Oberon.

TITANIA: I could sit in it, and sort of bend over inside the frame.

CYPRIAN: Actually, with a bit of luck it should be possible. But I serve Oberon.

TITANIA: And where I'm too thin you could pad it out.

CYPRIAN: If you give me the Black Boy in return.

TITANIA: Black boy, black boy. I don't know what you're talking about. What do I want with him? I no longer want any boy, or man. I, Pasiphae, am no longer interested in mundane, domestic intercourse!

CYPRIAN: You'll give me Norman and renounce your influence on him. You promise?

TITANIA: I promise. Whatever was once dear to me I gladly renounce. If you will effect the necessary improvements.
I see what he sees, tree and lake and fields.
My nights henceforth are white, as he is white.
His whiteness, wedding-whiteness blinds my eyes.
I want to make him happy, nothing more
So he'll come back to me.
Happy 'til his very horn-tips tingle.
I wish we were so close, so intertwined
That all my blood would sing with it, with him.

SCENE 11

In the park. HELMA has become a tree from the waist down. GEORGE is hugging her trunk.

GEORGE: Wolf loves Helen, loves not you.
You're squandering your finest years.

HELMA: No I blossom every year, I burgeon and bud with new green shoots. I give shade, I shield against winds and foul weather, I whisper, I groan. I am fertile – but not with him. I offer him stability and strength, unflinching loyalty, a healthy pace of life. Nor need he fear my getting old or being barren – I get through all that in the space of a year and then I'm back by his side, as young and fresh as ever

I was, ready to excite his love anew. So he has no cause to shrink from my temporary age, has he? I'm only odd and old and gnarled and cracked for a little while. Then I'm young again.

GEORGE: I must have been out of my mind, marrying Helen. Her body was all I saw. It was like some magnificent city gate and I strode through in triumph. But past the gate was the most horrible stinking shitheap of a place. I learned from my disappointment though – suddenly grew up. Now reason and desire walk hand in hand: you are the better woman, you're the one I need.

HELMA: Just because I can't hang onto the only man I love there's no reason to mock me for it.

GEORGE: Why would I mock? I dream about you all the time. Your mouth, your eyes, your sweet soft sadness. Your face encompasses my own. So when I smile, when I moan, I feel I'm you… Ah. My eyes are swimming with you. Your hands. I must lie down and rest. Being in love with you exhausts me.

(*HELMA disappears from the tree. Shortly after, HELEN enters from behind the hedge.*)

Ah, Helma what a dream was here.

I dreamt you were walking barefoot through

A field on the ears of corn,

You were so light, and so happy.

As you walked away…

HELEN: How dare you tell me all this crap you dreamt while sleeping with someone else.

GEORGE: Sometimes you look completely lost.

HELEN: So were you pretending all the time? That doesn't make sense. To love someone 'til yesterday, and today to leave them flat. That's a nasty little game to play.

GEORGE: You were all goodness, your sudden change of character drove you and me apart, and then forced two people, hitherto indifferent, into each other's hearts. Now we're in love.

HELEN: You call that love! At least with me you had to take some risks! Instead you've settled for the babbling brook, the cosy nook, the dinner table, the dashboard.

GEORGE: As you wish, Helen. But things were never right between us. When I kiss your mouth what nightmare ideas am I embracing? Yesterday racism, today belief in God, tomorrow superstition, magic, the Dark Ages, the day after…cannibalism for all I know!

HELEN: It's so easy to say things were never right between us. But now you've gone and lost your heart. Is that so bloody 'right'?

(*She exits behind the hedge. Enter HELMA.*)

HELMA: What's this thing doing to me? I'm suddenly so popular, which immediately makes me suspicious. I don't want to be sceptical but I must discover the truth. Perhaps I should just enjoy it – deceive myself and let others deceive me. No, not that. I'd be back to square one and none the wiser…

GEORGE: (*Enters.*) 'Who would not change a raven for a dove.' You are a dove, aren't you. You've no idea how my desire for you has chopped you into little bits. The parts I can't possess, can only dream of: breasts, thighs, hip. Off goes your head, off go your feet. A sex fiend with a chainsaw does not slay with half the lust of my fantasies of you.

HELMA: What are you saying? I'm afraid! I've only had one goal in life and that's to make my husband happy.

GEORGE: But you never have.

(*WOLF appears from behind the hedge.*)

Wolf! An apt name for my best friend.

WOLF: Listen, keep your Helen. I'll none of her. The scales have fallen from my eyes. She's not the one for me. A landslide of emotion – then she'd disappeared. If I ever loved her all that love is gone. Mystery it ever happened in the first place. Look, sorry, nothing personal, old chap… but I'll be going home a happier man.

GEORGE: So you want to stay with Helma? (*To himself.*) Shit.

HELMA: (*To GEORGE.*) Don't believe him! He's juggling with words… And so are you!

GEORGE: I'm not juggling. He's pretending, not me.

HELMA: You obviously need to make up some fake quarrel to get yourselves sexed up for Helen's bed.

GEORGE: Look, I'll ask you once more: Are you going to stay with Helma here?

WOLF: Yes, why not? She's pleasant enough.

GEORGE: Pleasant enough! Whatever happened to 'I love you' – such passion, such worship. Helma, what do you make of this half-hearted homecoming?

HELMA: Even if the half-hearted man spoke half the truth, I'd still jump for joy.

WOLF: I'm tired of searching. No more swapping. Now I know where I belong. You obviously can't imagine what it's like, to be married to such a woman, such a wife. Her lovely warm body so round, so firm. She's also so intelligent, so impulsive: what more could a man want?

HELMA: This Helma sounds fantastic. You must give me her phone number!

GEORGE: I know your tricks. Pretending to prefer her. You're just trying to make things harder for me.

WOLF: Oh yes and don't think I don't know what you're up to. You and Helma? Come on, you should be ashamed of yourself. Darling, don't listen to him.
(*HELEN enters suddenly.*)
I know for sure, she's told me. (*He means HELEN.*) He's just pretending in order to make her jealous, trying to shock her out of her sick philosophy.

HELEN: Don't believe him. I know the truth. He's crazy about you. He isn't faking.

HELMA: I see. You're part of this confederacy. You've conjoined all three to bait me with this…foul derision. What have I ever done to you that you should be so horrible?

HELEN: Done to you? You steal my closest friends and then you come on like the injured party!

HELMA: That isn't true. You set him on to me. You're all in it together to drive me mad. So I'm some sort of aphrodisiac to make you three love each other more. At least I'm a proper woman and not some anorexic reptile like you.

WOLF: That's enough! I see it now. You, Helma, are my wife, my only love, my life.

HELEN: Come on, don't make fun of her. He was much more
passionate when he was wooing me.
GEORGE: Shut your mouth and stay out of it, you...you
fucking niggerwhore.
(*HELEN stifles a cry.*)
HELMA: It's all right. He's only trying to get you turned on...
He wants you.
HELEN: Aha! So you know him better than me, do you?
WOLF: Aren't you overdoing it a bit?
GEORGE: Sod off and mind you own bloody business. Stick to
your line. I'll stick to mine.
HELMA: Hey you, I'm actually sticking up for you and you
don't even bloody notice.
HELEN: Sticking out more like! What good's a fat horse-turd
like you going to do me?
HELMA: I'm nice enough not to mind that men seem to find
your morbid brain attractive, somehow overlooking the
fact that you're built like an ironing board.
HELEN: Thanks for being so boring and so fat I'll smash your
stupid face in.
HELMA: Come on men, hold her back.
Don't assume I'm stronger.
I haven't got her wiry muscles.
HELEN: Men? You call them men?
Men have to learn to wage wars
Before they know how to love a woman.
Men must build empires, dice with Death,
Before they can even sense what women are.
You're enemies, right? Then act like enemies,
You want this woman, go on fight for her.
Does no one want to conquer anymore?
To tear another man apart, to know, for once
In your lives to know how a woman, taken in
Triumph, can love.
But you just can't do it, can you?
You talk it over, agreeing to agree.
Yes everything's arranged nowadays,
And everything that once was masculine,

Bone and marrow, sinew and cartilage,
Has atrophied to rotten jelly,
In these rotten times of peace.
Rotten! Rotten! Rotten!

GEORGE: That's enough, woman. And now get out of here.
I don't want you around me any more. Your every word
drives us further apart. I'm not obliged, as a man, or as a
member of society to share my life with a neo-Nazi. You've
gone completely mad.

HELEN: I've followed you a long, long way, my Lord. For
love. So don't complain that I've been driven mad. First
I was mad for you – then it consumed me. I've never
spared you any of my feelings. None. But now I'll take my
madness and carry it away, very carefully, I'll take it out of
town. And bury it deep in a sealed container – so it won't
contaminate anybody anymore.

(*OBERON shouts from above: 'Cyprian, Cyprian!' One half of the
stage is lit. On a bank we see TITANIA lying on a bloodstained
sheet. She has the hindquarters of a cow. The THREE BOYS and
the FIRST GIRL are standing around her. As are FIRSTLING,
the miniature COURTLING and the BLACK BOY. HELMA,
GEORGE and WOLF slowly join. HELEN stays sitting by the
hedge. TITANIA creeps and slides around helplessly on the sheet.
She's panting, saying something that might almost be 'Send the
children away. I don't want the children to see me...' CYPRIAN
appears among them.*)

SCENE 12

OBERON: Cyprian, what have you done?
The whole house reeks of your negligence.
And everything around you's been screwed up.
Nothing but dissent and separation. Look!
The petals of true love are black with blight,
And rotten. People who can't stand each other
Are catapulted together with false desire.

CYPRIAN: Didn't you complain that humankind
Had squandered all its passion and its lust?

I heeded what you said. And then *created* –
I did it in your image, in your name.

OBERON: Cyprian, Cyprian. What have you done?
Who gave you permission to try my magic out
On ordinary people – and to spread it
Out to every corner of the world?
For one assignment only I gave you
This special gift, revealed this ancient secret.
Which you abused by taking nature's spirits
And mass producing them.

CYPRIAN: Why shouldn't I turn talent into profit?
Why should I grow old and bitter as a failure?
Genius deserves success; you should have guessed
The magic having worked so well, that I
Would want to keep on making miracles.

OBERON: You weren't supposed to. It wasn't allowed.
My trust has been criminally abused.

CYPRIAN: Criminal, criminal. It's a strong word.
I'm used to a rather simpler morality.

OBERON: Yes I noticed. You take what is not yours.
To take, and reap what you did not sow.

CYPRIAN: Much of it is what I made of it.
You wouldn't have got very far without me.

OBERON: Curse your creative talent,
You did not see my reasons, or the need.
Get rid of the amulets, all the talismans,
Throw them away, good people!

CYPRIAN: What have I done wrong?
Sir, I was only doing my best.

OBERON: Exactly, and your best was bad enough.
You can't awake the grey primeval force
In somebody who cannot live with it.
Or rouse up naked lust in those who are
Still constricted in their minds.

CYPRIAN: Why should I care if their lives are out of joint? I
can't change that. I merely offer them a gift, add a bit of
spice to their pathetic lives. And people are grateful. So if
my work has proved popular, then I'm thrilled. Time is

the only master here on earth, sir, and I'm proud to be its willing slave.

OBERON: Titania's been turned into a blood-soaked myth. Instead of being rigorously soothed and tamed with solemn ceremony – she's gone berserk. She lies mutilated clamouring for her bull. A nightmare gatecrasher from another age, the direct result of your after-care. Oh no, I wanted to see their faces aglow with intelligent desire, not with this lascivious, self-lacerating love.

CYPRIAN: I serve you, my Lord, and gladly. But not you alone. Now I am the servant of the people. I've got a new master that is equally demanding.

OBERON: Then satisfy your lust for success! If you have got
Any talent left, use it now.
I here renounce my influence on you,
And sever the connection of our powers.
Then I will undergo a transformation,
And even if I run the risk of never
Being Oberon again – I quit my post.
I'll be a miserable bastard like the rest,
A fellow sufferer in the general sorrow.
So take my power, my name, all I possess,
Disseminate the essence of my being
Like dust, into the air these earthlings breathe.
Maybe it will work, perhaps the world
Will be improved a bit. And maybe not.
In any case henceforth I'll be a man like Cyprian.
No more, no less. I hereby discharge myself.
(OBERON disappears. ALL leave separately. TITANIA crawls wearily on. GEORGE passes HELEN.)

HELEN: George!

GEORGE: Yes?

HELEN: Couldn't everything stay the way it was?

GEORGE: Helen…

HELEN: All right, all right.

Blackout.

Act Four

SCENE 1

The next morning. WOLF and HELMA lie entwined, asleep. Lower down sits TITANIA in a light coat, modern dress. Next to her the cow frame and her historical costume. She looks at this debris in amazement. Gets up, looks a bit closer – sits down again. Above, asleep, FIRSTLING next to COURTLING, now normal size. From the right comes OBERON. He is wearing a suit and smoking a cigarette. He bows to the others and introduces himself: 'Middlemass.' But no one can hear. He saws the air with the hand with the cigarette in it, as if soliloquising. 'I'm too quiet,' he mutters. 'I haven't got the full sound yet.' He goes back. He tries his entrance again, with similar results. 'There's no point, they can't hear me. I don't impinge.' Meanwhile, CYPRIAN, also in a suit, crosses the stage and exits. He has a metre rule and scissors, measuring and checking everything he comes across, from the twig protruding from the hedge to the loop on his own waistband, which he cuts off. 'Doesn't fit.' – meaning his clothing – 'Doesn't fit.' Whatever he's measuring – 'Nothing fits anymore.' – recalcitrance this time. 'Nothing fits at all.' TITANIA makes up, combs her hair, looking at her reflection in her compact. WOLF and HELMA wake up. They blink their eyes and spring apart.

OBERON: Middlemass, Middlemass.

CYPRIAN: It doesn't fit.

OBERON: I'm too quiet, not the full sound yet.

CYPRIAN: It doesn't fit.

OBERON: Middlemass, Middlemass. No point they can't hear me. I don't impinge. (*Exit.*)

CYPRIAN: It doesn't fit, doesn't fit. Nothing fits at all. Nothing fits anymore.

WOLF: What happened? Why have you got your arms around me?

HELMA: I woke up and your arms were around me.

WOLF: What's happened?

HELMA: Don't know. Has something happened?

WOLF: It's never happened to me before. Not even when I was drunk.

HELMA: Well perhaps something has happened,
    And I can't even remember what it was.
    Perhaps there was something,
    I've had a complete blackout.
    (*She gets up – takes off her jacket.*)
WOLF: What's that hanging around your neck?
HELMA: Ugh! Oh yes, 'The Thing'.
WOLF: Disgusting.
HELMA: Things go out of fashion so quickly.
WOLF: Chuck it away.
HELMA: Hey. It was expensive.
WOLF: Get rid of it.
    (*She tears it off and throws it into the hedge. Both exit.*
    FIRSTLING wakes up next to COURTLING.)
FIRSTLING: Hallo little chap. Look at you reading the morning
    paper just like a grown-up. I bet you don't understand a
    word of it, do you?
COURTLING: Apparently they've developed another new fruit.
    This one's a cross between an aubergine and a tomato.
    Why can't they just leave things alone?
    (*FIRSTLING gets up, peers over the paper.*)
FIRSTLING: Courtling?
COURTLING: Yes.
FIRSTLING: The dream's over. I knew it, one day, it'd be over.
COURTLING: What are you talking about?
FIRSTLING: My God, how quickly one can grow fond of a
    sweet little fellow like him… His little hand in mine – so he
    didn't cross the road when the light was red.
COURTLING: Nobody needs architects anymore. It makes me
    sick to the stomach.
    (*He gets up, chucks FIRSTLING the newspaper, exits.*)
FIRSTLING: Hey, you great lummox, wait for me.
    (*He runs after him. TITANIA goes to the hedge; disappears into*
    it. CYPRIAN enters, stands next to the hedge.)
CYPRIAN: Oberon? Can you hear me? Oberon?
TITANIA: Not here.
CYPRIAN: Titania?
TITANIA: Not here.
CYPRIAN: Cobweb, Moth, Peaseblossom?

TITANIA: Not here, not here.

CYPRIAN: Not here, not here. Heaven, Earth, Moonshine Overseas, Man-child?

TITANIA: Not here, not here, not here.

(*Exit CYPRIAN. The SECOND BOY climbs on stage. He strokes TITANIA's costume then sort of jumps on it. In front of the hedge stands the FIRST GIRL, arms out sideways as if she was supporting herself against a wall. She shouts to passers-by: 'Pig!' or 'Cow!' The following pass by: GEORGE, HELMA with WOLF's jacket over her arm. Finally OBERON. As they are shouted at they stumble or jump to one side. OBERON stands stock-still next to the hedge, covering his face with his hands. The SECOND BOY walks forward with TITANIA's costume.*)

FIRST GIRL: Pig!

SECOND BOY: Calm down.

FIRST GIRL: (*Pointing at OBERON.*) That bloke's my dad!

(*FIRST and SECOND BOYS jump out from behind the hedge, holding their lighted cigarette-lighters up to OBERON's jacket pockets.*)

FIRST BOY: Hey, dad! Dad!

THIRD BOY: Hey, dad. Have another fag!

FIRST BOY: Yeah, dad. Have another fag!

THIRD BOY: (*Splashing beer on the singed material.*) Have another drink, dad.

FIRST BOY: 'Nother beer. Come on dad.

FIRST GIRL: Nico? Are you mad? Yeah, he's fucking disgusting. He's pissed on her dress. He's done shit on her dress – messed it up.

SECOND BOY: You've got it all worked out, don't you? But just you wait. Any day now you're going to get the shock of your life. Empty. It's all empty. But you wait. Actually I knew her quite well. Well, she sent me this letter, didn't she?

SCENE 2 – TROY

Deserted. A small triangular space, asphalt floor. A wooden fence painted red-black-gold. Sticking out of the floor, a radio-antenna with German flag on top. WOLF presses his ear to the asphalt and hears a mixture of accordion music and political speeches, which crackles distortedly, out

of the ground. HELMA nearby on a chair, WOLF's jacket on her lap.
OBERON/MIDDLEMASS walks up and down behind her, along the fence,
smoking a cigarette.

HELMA: It's beyond me. How can a grown man get so
completely bound up in his own fatherland? What is it for
God's sake that moves him, a burnt-out case like him, to
tears when someone strikes that note, that precise note of
'Germanness'. It'll always be a mystery to me. 'I love you
my native land, my poor proud fatherland, I love you…'
But I'm glad it's still being broadcast. The only thing that
moves him, the Nation. Apart from that no flow in the
blood – stagnant. The only way he can reclaim something
of himself is through that particular sound, that odd distant
crackling sound. So I'm glad it's still being broadcast. For
how much longer, who knows? Only first thing, though.
Fatherland-fans, like him, have to get up early. He wouldn't
look half so happy if I wasn't sitting next to him. He says
so himself. So it's nice to feel you're not entirely useless.
What'll happen if they stop broadcasting it? Direct from
Troy, from the deepest depths, no more sounds, no more
messages. I wouldn't be able to keep him, I'm sure of it.
I wouldn't have the strength. Not on my own. We don't
even hold hands any more. Why should we after all these
years? So nothing is shared, nothing is held. He doesn't
hold my hand, I don't hold his. Even the slightest move in
that direction – it would all be over. If we did hold hands,
I can't imagine ever having any other feeling than, that's
it – over. Irrevocably. Over and done with. 'Farewell, my
love.' 'Farewell, my darling.' These words would be the
natural consequence of any touch of the hand. Completely
automatically. No hard feelings, but there we go. The
slightest bit of hand-holding and those words would bubble
forth like a natural spring, silvery, as clear as crystal. Yes
that would be it – a clear water separation. No ifs, no buts.
Even if he fell and couldn't get up off the ground. I'd come
up from behind, get myself under his arms and sort of
lever him up with my knee in the small of his back. I've
got it all worked out. I'd never approach from the front

and pull him up by the hands. I can no longer bring myself to look at him from the front. I just can't do it. If I did, oh, how lovely, how strange it would be to look him in the eyes – we used to be so open with each other. Once. Now, out of the question. The same thing: from the front, eye to eye, touch of the hand, farewell, over and done with. It's a completely logical sequence. One thing automatically follows the other. So I protect myself. We both protect ourselves. We sit around like crows, next to each other, enjoying the same view. But face to face – and it would be over. Irrevocably. If we faced each other, then that would be that. Even the slightest hint of eye contact would be a sure sign of separation. I'm sure it would all happen in a flash. A look, a step closer, a touch of the hand, farewell. One thing follows the next. Over and done with. Even if he'd been shopping and came back with two heavy bags and I'd have to open the front door for him, I'd always do it with my head bowed, like I was suddenly fascinated by these gorgeous shopping bags. I've been prepared for that one for a while now. But I'd never hold my head up and ask if he's remembered the fresh meringues, which we do need fresh every morning, actually, which he always seems to forget, and always really misses when they're not there. But imagine – to *ask* him something! That's the surest way to set off an unstoppable chain reaction. Question, look, step, hand, over. If I did ask – what an unforgettable delight! A simple, modern, affectionate question, and to get a profound, ancient answer back. God, what wouldn't I give to feel, once more, from top to toe, with every inch of me, to feel *answered*! I'm afraid my poor little ears would glow like coals and swell up like cockscombs... But God what am I thinking of? The slightest hint of an answer and that's it. Finito. The end. That's why the last thing I'd do is ask him a question. If there has to be talk, it's to ourselves. If hands, then our own. If looks, then in the same direction, if you don't mind. Anything else would be tantamount to suicide. I can hear him, oh yes. Going on about the fatherland. And I'd like to think he hears me too. So it's not as if we don't get anything from each other. We

just leave each other in peace. In a big way. I don't love
the fatherland like he does. I love him. And if we want to
make it, well we've just got to keep going...like we have up
to now...

(*OBERON/MIDDLEMASS advances, speaks kindly but silently to
them both. WOLF steps back and takes HELMA's hand.*)

SCENE 3

*The BLACK BOY enters. CYPRIAN produces a box from his pocket, opens
it and takes out a figure, holds it out in his outstretched hand.*

CYPRIAN: Look. For you. Obscene isn't it? (*Laughs.*)
Amazingly obscene, eh? For you. I made it for you. There!
(*The BLACK BOY knocks it out of his hand. Annoyed, CYPRIAN
bends over to look for it.*)
It's broken... You filthy bastard.
(*The BLACK BOY puts his foot on CYPRIAN's side, kicks him
over, quite gently.*)
No, no... I've got money. I've got money too. Here,
money, loads of it. Come here, look, count it, count the
money.
(*The BLACK BOY kneels down and takes the money out of
CYPRIAN's pocket. Suddenly CYPRIAN takes the big scissors and
holds them against the BLACK BOY's neck.*)
Do it. Do it.
(*Pushes the BOY's head down. The BLACK BOY pulls down
CYPRIAN's trousers.*)
Do it. Do it.
(*Suddenly the BLACK BOY knocks the scissors out of CYPRIAN's
hand. Takes a stone which he smashes repeatedly into CYPRIAN's
face. CYPRIAN holds his head, limbs flailing. Then freezes
suddenly. The BLACK BOY runs off. Partial blackout.
Suddenly, right, we see the suburban house in which HELEN is
now living. Almost empty room, table, chair, wash-stand with
a jug and bowl. A sofa-bed. A hooded man in a black Parka,
black jeans, black shoes slowly leaves the room. HELEN, on the
sofa, suddenly sits upright. Blackout.*)

Then, left, we hear shouts. WOLF – 'The sculptor's been murdered!' Voices young and old join in, staccato cries like you hear on ski-slopes, 'Ho, ho, ho, ho, ho!' WOLF, against the growing chorus: 'What are you shouting? I don't understand what you've saying.' The CHORUS bursts into laughter. Lights. OBERON is standing next to CYPRIAN. Who is dead.

OBERON: It's not what I intended, Cyprian.

It's not what I intended.

But I couldn't prevent it.

I'm no longer your lord,

I'm merely your stupid, mumbling friend.

I can do nothing any more.

The game, which I invented, inevitably

Led to my own destruction.

The battle's over, Titania, Love has lost.

Make sure that you can escape from Time.

Or his long arm will get you in the end.

For me, it's now too late.

My power, my fame are hollow things.

Trampled in the dust,

And blown about by the wind.

Hither

And thither.

SCENE 4

HELEN in her house. Obscene graffiti on the walls. She is with THE MAN IN BLACK – DEATH. You can only see his back. And he is seated; his bony fingers rest on his knees.

DEATH: Did you send for me?

HELEN: No. No I did not.

DEATH: That's odd. (*He makes as if to go.*)

HELEN: No, stay. Have you always been as terrifying as you are now?

(*DEATH shrugs.*)

Do you want to warn me that I should lead a better life?

Do you want me to…in spite of everything, to take you in my arms?

DEATH: I don't have a lot to say. I don't do much. I'm just sort of here. And I've always been the same, representing nothing in particular – but I've always been amazed that nobody looks at me.

HELEN: But you are Death. You have the power.

DEATH: Don't you believe it.

HELEN: You make yourself man-sized – you make yourself loveable – just to win me for yourself? It's quiet here, isn't it?

DEATH: Yes.

HELEN: Very quiet. Every morning when the sun creeps over the hill, I still think, 'The postman will be coming soon, they'll be getting up next door.' But there's none of that here. The sun could be riding a big dipper in the sky and it would be the same down here, just as quiet.

DEATH: Yes.

HELEN: So, you are nothingness. Just this little man.

(*DEATH giggles a bit.*)

All that screaming. All that big silly fuss. And then he comes, then he comes along, our little friend.

DEATH: Yes. That's the way it happens.

HELEN: Where are the leaping flames, the trapdoors? Where's the evil?

DEATH: Yeah, well. It could be worse, couldn't it?

(*He stands up.*)

HELEN: Don't come too close!

SCENE 5 – PEOPLE OF HIS SORT

TITANIA on the gallery. Below THREE YOUNG MEN in white sports kit. The FIRST MAN is just taking his white flannels off. The SECOND MAN is doing up his white shoes, the THIRD MAN is pulling his sweater off his head. They stay in these poses as TITANIA calls down to them.

TITANIA: One of you, who are alike as three well-packed snowballs, is actually my beloved, my lord – the way you're standing I can't recognise which one. He has a voice like gold, and a good head of hair. I know that he's hidden himself among people similar to you three sportsmen. So speak – you first, man trying to take his flannels off.

73

FIRST MAN: Well, I do have a voice of gold, and a good head of hair. But I've never been in love in my life. So it can't be me.

TITANIA: Now you speak, man doing up his shoelace.

SECOND MAN: I've also got a voice of gold. And indeed a good head of hair. But I've got a wife and two children at home. So obviously I can't be the one you're after.

TITANIA: Now you speak, man pulling sweater over his head.

THIRD MAN: I don't need to speak, because I don't have a voice of gold.

TITANIA: Sorry. Would take your sweater off so I can hear properly. I have a suspicion you might be him.

(*He pulls his sweater from his head, but not from his arms.*)

TITANIA: Now speak.

THIRD MAN: I don't have a voice of gold – so it can't be me.

TITANIA: Now that's what I call a voice of gold! Don't be so modest – you do yourself no favours. You don't need to hide with the others. And you've got a good head of hair. So. Sweaterman, trouserman, shoelaceman. One of you must be the one. I know it. But because my beloved, my unseen joy, knows the way to blind me with lying and deceit, I will ask you no further questions. So, I warn you. Step forward on your own and make yourself known. Beware, for it is in my power to tell your two friends what a disaster you are, what a slob, what a wimp. I don't need to tell them what a deceiver you are – they can see for themselves. Right. I'm waiting. You. Step forward sweaterman – you're the one.

THIRD MAN: Who? Me?

TITANIA: Who else? Did you think I wouldn't recognize you, standing there, hiding your face, sweater over your head? Oh, my only love.

THIRD MAN: Why me of all people?

TITANIA: Ha! Typical. Still ringing in my ears, 'Why me of all people?' How many times have I heard that. Every time you ask him to get the wine, to put flowers on the table. So adorably bad-mannered!

THIRD MAN: Hang on, hang on. Even if, and I say if, I could possibly be your beloved, I'm completely baffled why the finger of suspicion should point so unambiguously at me. What's so terribly particular about me that should rule out both these other gentlemen?

TITANIA: Trouserman! Do you know that man?

FIRST MAN: Who? Sweaterman?

TITANIA: Yes.

FIRST MAN: I met him for the first time just now. Out on the pitch.

SECOND MAN: And I met both of them just now, out on the pitch.

TITANIA: Heavens above, you're getting me completely confused. How should I know how I'm supposed to find you, you elusive god? 'Apollo flies and Daphne holds the chase. The story shall be changed.' I want our dissent to end happily: I love you.

SECOND MAN: Um...whom do you mean now?

TITANIA: You!

SECOND MAN: Not me, please, don't get me into trouble.

TITANIA: Trouserman! I want to ask you something. Answer me in all honesty. Everything depends on it. You told me you had never been in love. Well, look at me. (*She opens her coat.*) Look at me. Look at all of me. Look, wherever you want to look. Good. And now I will ask the question: could you ever fall in love with me?

FIRST MAN: Now I'm confused. I've never seen anything so beautiful in a human being. And I have to speak as I feel, I have to say 'yes'.

TITANIA: You, shoelace. You have a wife and children. Would you take me nonetheless?

SECOND MAN: You know I never lie – my answer is 'yes'.

TITANIA: Sweater. Given you could conquer your shyness.

THIRD MAN: God help me, you'd only have to walk a pace towards me and straight away I'd say 'yes'.

TITANIA: So each of you would be prepared to take me as a lover. One of you is the meanest lying bastard who ever walked this God-forsaken earth. And I've one more thing to say to penetrate his heart: Midsummer Night. That's all. He knows what I mean. You see. Now he's gone all pale. (*The THREE MEN look at each other.*)

And you two, the other two who are shielding him,
protecting him with your ludicrous similarity. What am I to
do with you?

THIRD MAN: I'm not shielding anyone. I'm not protecting
anyone. I promise.

SECOND MAN: If I find the scoundrel I'll hand him over.

FIRST MAN: I don't know either of you gentlemen. But
something the lady said also occurred to me. That you're
both identical, almost interchangeable.

THIRD MAN: You have the nerve to say that when you're so
like this gentleman here, you could be twins.

FIRST MAN: I think I can say, in all conscience, that I'm the
only one who doesn't look like anyone else here.

SECOND MAN: That's just where you're wrong. I was thinking
just now, when I came in: blow me, you and the other
gentleman are like two peas in a pod.

FIRST MAN: Do you think that I resemble you, as much as this
other gentleman, who by the way is your double, seems to
claim?

THIRD MAN: No. Not a bit. I don't see it at all.

FIRST MAN: Well then. If I don't look anything like you, and if
you and this gentleman could be twins, then it follows that
I'm the only one here who couldn't be mistaken for either
of the others.

SECOND MAN: But you look just like him. Whereas I can't
see why you refer to him as my double. I don't look like
anyone else.

TITANIA: Enough. You are incapable of finding him out, the
seeming stranger, the fraud, who's pretending not to know
every inch of me by heart. Then it is incumbent on me to
discover the joker in this heartless pack of men. Listen. You
all told me, all three, that you would take me as a lover.

ALL THREE MEN: Yes, you bet, like a shot.

TITANIA: But what would your reaction be if I became not
only your lover, but also that of you other two rascals here?
(*The THREE MEN make the sounds of second thoughts. 'Oh, oh,'
says one; the other sucks his teeth and shakes his head sceptically.
The third tut-tuts in a disappointed way.*)
Would you be prepared to fight to the *death* to win me?

76

FIRST MAN: I don't really think so. Do you?

SECOND MAN: Not necessarily.

THIRD MAN: That might be going a bit far. I mean nowadays.

TITANIA: I see. So it wouldn't be a complete catastrophe for any of you, not to have me?

FIRST MAN: No. Not a complete catastrophe, I wouldn't call it that.

SECOND MAN: Bad luck. Sheer bad luck.

THIRD MAN: A pity, definitely, but there you go.

TITANIA: Well, you will not be mollified, great guardian of my joy. They spoke with one mouth, and it was yours my Lord, wonderful and weary and cruel. You have become unrecognisable, and I will never find you. So I give up. I have not seen you and thus I cannot say to you the most important thing I've ever had to say to anyone. For it is something that you alone must know. Believe me, it's not some mundane secret whispered by a woman desperately trying to make herself more interesting. No, my gift to you was a truth, which you would have used well. It would have been of great value to you. More I cannot say. It wasn't just a word, just sound and breath, but amounted to a thing, a thing of beauty, of quite exceptional beauty… But now you will not have it. I kiss you. Fare you well.
(*She exits. The THREE MEN stand in a row, facing away from us, hands behind their backs. The man in the middle has no glove on his right hand. The other two lean slightly back and notice his uneasy, naked hand. Their gaze wanders upwards and they scrutinize the odd man out.*)

SCENE 6

GEORGE and WOLF in the park. WOLF hands GEORGE a pair of binoculars.

WOLF: You see that house over there?

GEORGE: Yes.

WOLF: No, hang on a second. Someone's turned a light on.

GEORGE: Helen!… Where is she? Where is that house? Who's that dark bloke next to her? I must go to her.

WOLF: Don't interfere.

GEORGE: She's standing at the window, looking out. As if she could see me.

WOLF: She can't. We're too far away.

GEORGE: But it's as if she were looking for me in her mind. She's got someone for dinner.

WOLF: Looks like he's quite at home there.

GEORGE: They're leaning over the dinner table. Hands almost touching. I've got to go to her.

WOLF: No. Stay. It's pointless. Don't interrupt her.

GEORGE: 'Don't interrupt her'! Doing what? Who is that guy? I'll smash his face in.

WOLF: I don't think you will.

GEORGE: Who is he? What's his name?

WOLF: Death.

GEORGE: Oh yes? First name?

WOLF: No, George. 'Death'.

GEORGE: Don't talk rubbish. Where's he live? Where can I get hold of him? Prat, dressed in black.

WOLF: You want to try to take him on? Ha!

GEORGE: I'll get him out the way. You'll see.

WOLF: Yes, you try it. Just you try it…

SCENE 7

HELEN alone in the house. She gets up from the sofa. On the cover the black imprint of a skeleton. She goes to the wash-stand and washes.

SCENE 8

Park. GEORGE, dishevelled, covered with black spots. Enter WOLF.

GEORGE: I couldn't get a real grip on him.

WOLF: He gave you a good going over.

GEORGE: If I'd got a grip on him, he'd be just a pile of bones by now.

WOLF: Let's face it – he demolished you.

GEORGE: No wonder! If you can't get a grip on someone you can't throw them properly.

WOLF: So let's at least admit it. Helen's got the stronger man.

GEORGE: A great comfort you are. Yes thanks a bunch, that makes me feel a lot better. And where were you? Hiding behind the hedge!

WOLF: I did warn you. Told you not to interfere. I know, she's not to be interrupted – not while she's tussling with Mr Big.

GEORGE: And he's a bloody ghost. What do I do? Do you think this will last for long? I want to put a question to you, Wolf. Do you think that our death, by which I mean Death for us men, well, will it be a woman?

WOLF: Strictly speaking it has to be a She. Black hair, black breasts. I don't know how I'd feel if it was any different. You know, your last moment on earth, and this bloke turns up!

GEORGE: I've been bitterly unfair to Helen. Her heart bled for me. I have wronged someone, Wolf.

WOLF: I can see that you are tortured by remorse.

GEORGE: You can see it – but you don't see the extent of it. The guilt!

SCENE 9

COURTLING and FIRSTLING.

COURTLING: For God's sake leave your cigarette case alone.

FIRSTLING: It's driving me bonkers. It won't shut.

COURTLING: What have you got in there?

FIRSTLING: A scarf.

COURTLING: You shouldn't put a scarf inside a cigarette case.

FIRSTLING: It's a silk scarf.

COURTLING: One of your mother's silk scarves?

FIRSTLING: Well of course, you twit. It's hardly one of mine.

COURTLING: Do you seriously think you can shut that bit of cloth inside that cigarette case?

FIRSTLING: Of course I can. You can fold it so thin it'll fit perfectly.

COURTLING: But you can see yourself it doesn't fit at all.

FIRSTLING: It always has done.

COURTLING: But now it's popped open and it won't shut any more.

FIRSTLING: They are two mementoes of my mother: and they belong together. Damn and blast it!

COURTLING: It's popped open. Maybe she's thinking of you…

FIRSTLING: Nonsense. Stupid bloody thing.

COURTLING: Let me have a go.

FIRSTLING: Hey, hands off.

COURTLING: Not stupid, it's pretty. It's a present from your mother.

FIRSTLING: Don't.

COURTLING: Looks like a gaping wound, with the red cloth…

FIRSTLING: Stop talking such irresponsible complete bloody rubbish.

COURTLING: You're treating me as if I was the cigarette case.

FIRSTLING: You're certainly a darn sight more irritating than the damn thing.

COURTLING: My dear chap, I'm sorry, but I bear absolutely no resemblance to this cigarette case.

FIRSTLING: I never said you looked like a cigarette case. All I'm saying is that you're every bit as irritating as this particular cigarette case.

COURTLING: Even *in extremis* I think one should have the decency to differentiate between a friend and a cigarette case.

FIRSTLING: I don't see that much difference. They're both close to my heart, and they both get on my nerves.

COURTLING: I'm not some sort of cigarette case you can stuff with neatly folded insults and then just snap shut and put back in your pocket. I won't let you just put me back in your pocket.

FIRSTLING: The comparison wasn't with a cigarette case you can snap shut. I wasn't saying that. I compared you to an expensive cigarette case which won't close, and thus with a rare unfathomable object, endlessly fascinating, which one never tires of.

COURTLING: You have this infallible knack of fraudulently converting certain invidious comparisons retrospectively to your own advantage. Which is only possible because I am the weaker of the two, and that's because my innate good nature compels me to be more dependent on you than you are on me, um, you on me, yes. Which is why you think you can treat me like a cigarette case which always gives in eventually, and claim afterwards that in fact you were typifying me as something unfathomable, something which cannot be simply snapped shut. Which is an untruth. But I bow to you, you are the mightier. You can rewrite history. You can even rewrite the history of our friendship, so cleverly that in the end one would think that the cart had been pulling the horse...

SCENE 10

HELEN in her house. The MAN IN BLACK enters. HELEN jumps behind him and blindfolds him. He paws at the air, as if playing blind-man's buff. At last he sits down. She sits opposite. We hear voices: GEORGE, FIRSTLING and COURTLING.

GEORGE: Gentlemen! How's the sales manager thing going? Any progress?

FIRSTLING: I think we've found the right man, sir.

COURTLING: His name is Middlemass. Started off as a data-salesman.

FIRSTLING: He's making a very good impression. Not as young as he was though.

COURTLING: Everyone knows the older you get the less likely you are to survive this business.

(*They enter the house.*)

HELEN: (*Rising.*) George.

GEORGE: Good morning, my darling.

FIRSTLING/COURTLING: Good morning.

GEORGE: Let's go somewhere else, gentlemen. We'd better go somewhere else.

(*They wander off. HELEN sits down again. The MAN IN BLACK tries to undo his blindfold with his bony finger. In vain. He recognises his impotence.*)

Act Five

SCENE 1

All-night café. WOLF, HELMA, FIRSTLING, COURTLING, OBERON/
MIDDLEMASS at a table. Next door, GEORGE and HELEN. Behind,
the FIRST BOY and the FIRST GIRL, a BARMAN, who also waits on
tables.

WOLF: Middlemass, we've invited you here, although we've
    had an accident with you.

HELMA: You with us, more like.

WOLF: And although you've caused considerable damage to us
    and our car.

OBERON / MIDDLEMASS: (*Quietly.*) Not my fault.

WOLF: I beg your pardon.

HELMA: You be careful.

FIRSTLING: 'Not my fault,' he says.

WOLF: We thought we'd leave the question of who's to blame
    to one side for the time being.

HELMA: So we asked you out here so we can just relax and
    chat calmly about it in peace and quiet.

COURTLING: I sincerely hope your kind invitation isn't a
    clever way of wangling some sort of confession of guilt
    from him.

HELMA: Then you'd better keep your eye on us, hadn't you.

WOLF: Your boorish insinuations are not a very good start to
    this meeting.

HELEN: (*From the next-door table.*) Don't you like it?

WOLF: Well, you have to like green sauce.

OBERON / MIDDLEMASS: If green sauce it be.

WOLF: Sorry?

FIRSTLING: If green sauce it be.

WOLF: Anyway, you came zooming out of that parking space.

OBERON / MIDDLEMASS: (*Shakes his head.*) No.

WOLF: Look, you already admitted you had your eyes fixed
    on the intersection, and what's more, looking left although
    you were going right. So, my dear chap, the whole of the
    right-hand side of the road wasn't even in your eyeline.

OBERON / MIDDLEMASS: I was in the correct lane.

WOLF: I'm sorry?

FIRSTLING: He was in the correct lane, when *you* came zooming along.

WOLF: Look, I'm a driving instructor –

HELMA: You haven't always been…

OBERON / MIDDLEMASS: Wing flew off! Body work flew off! Fender flew off! Headlamp smashed! Front wheel off!

WOLF: Driver's wing mirror destroyed!

HELMA: Collision damage!

OBERON / MIDDLEMASS: Radiator grill flew off!

WOLF: Five yards into the air.

HELMA: Looks like a piece of modern art now.

OBERON / MIDDLEMASS: Picasso.

HELMA: We've just had the poor thing resprayed.

WOLF: We must include that in the replacement costs.

HELMA: Did you keep the receipt?

WOLF: Of course. Spray work. Respray work. Cost of replacement plus respray spray work.

HELMA: Any work on the rust?

WOLF: No, nothing.

(*Enter TITANIA.*)

COURTLING: Middlemass, get up. She's coming. Get on with it.

(*FIRSTLING, COURTLING, OBERON / MIDDLEMASS stand in a row opposite TITANIA. Silence.*)

TITANIA: Ah. Which one is it?

(*OBERON/MIDDLEMASS raises the index finger of his right hand. He and TITANIA go to each other. Arms round each other's necks they press their brows together.*)

Do you recognize me?

OBERON / MIDDLEMASS: Yes.

TITANIA: And does that make you happy?

OBERON / MIDDLEMASS: Yes.

TITANIA: How are you?

OBERON / MIDDLEMASS: Good.

TITANIA: Are those your friends?

OBERON / MIDDLEMASS: Yes.

TITANIA: Are they ill?

OBERON / MIDDLEMASS: No. They're dreaming. Just dreaming.

TITANIA: You're still a powerful man, aren't you?

OBERON / MIDDLEMASS: Yes.

TITANIA: And clever?

OBERON / MIDDLEMASS: Yes.

(*They sit at a table.*)

WOLF: Middlemass. Come here, will you. Make a sketch of the events of the accident. My good lady-wife and I will do the same.

OBERON / MIDDLEMASS: Yes.

(*He sits with the others. COURTLING gives him a pencil and paper. TITANIA can't take her eyes off him. She occasionally goes up to him, whispers something in his ear. He inclines his head, smiles contentedly. Or giggles a bit. You can see it by his shoulders. The BARMAN brings a glass of something. Bends down to OBERON/MIDDLEMASS.*)

BARMAN: Right. What's my name, what's my name?

OBERON / MIDDLEMASS: Your name is Martin Trowotzke.

BARMAN: Correct. You got it eventually. Three times I asked, three times you were stuck.

(*The FIRST BOY and the FIRST GIRL at their table.*)

FIRST GIRL: No listen. You don't understand, I'd had too much to drink. That's why there was some physical contact. And how!

FIRST BOY: That's no excuse. If a drunk driver has an accident they can have him up in court for it.

FIRST GIRL: I don't get guilt feelings.

FIRST BOY: But I fucking do. I know I feel guilty if something happens to me on the way home.

HELEN: (*Turns round to them.*) What are you saying? What are you saying?

GEORGE: Don't listen to them.

FIRST BOY: You're such a fucking whore!

FIRST GIRL: Who's a whore?

HELEN: It's offensive the way you're talking. You're offending me. Do you want to offend me, is that it?

FIRST BOY: Ha! And what about you offending us with your mega bank account and your big cars spewing out pollution?

HELEN: Excuse me, I can't offend you with my bank account, 'cause I haven't got one. Nor have I got a big car. I haven't got any sort of car.

GEORGE: Now, now.

FIRST GIRL: You called me a fucking whore. I don't have to take that from anyone.

(*She stands up, walks forward.*)

FIRST BOY: All right go on, piss off. You're not the only one with problems.

FIRST GIRL: (*Spits in front of OBERON/MIDDLEMASS.*) Ugh! Look at your face. Fucking ugly mug. Pfor! Shit! Christ!

OBERON / MIDDLEMASS: I don't know you. Please go.

(*FIRST BOY pulls her back.*)

Perhaps I am a singularly unprepossessing person.

HELEN: All the atrocities of all the wars ever won't be enough. No, only the eternal agonies of hell, when they come round again. That'll show you what's what.

FIRST BOY: Either you shut your mouth – or you present your arguments in proper debate form.

HELEN: (*Lost for a reply.*) Yes, well I –

GEORGE: Will you shut up!

HELEN: This great tide of weaklings may yet wash us all away… Except the devil might thin out our ranks a bit.

(*The FIRST BOY taps his forehead – as if to say: 'Mad!' – leaves with the FIRST GIRL.*)

GEORGE: Helen, what's all this about?

HELEN: After all I've been through the least I can expect is a bit of respect – and not to be made fun of.

GEORGE: But that boy has no idea what you've…

(*He tries to embrace her.*)

HELEN: I'm tired, George.

GEORGE: 'I'm tired.' Is that the new incantation to ward off evil spirits? 'Get thee behind me Satan. I'm tired.' Is that it?

HELEN: Why don't you understand me?

WOLF: I think this music's really awful.

TITANIA: (*To OBERON/MIDDLEMASS.*) Go on, try. Go on, see if you can do it. Look into the future.

GEORGE: Look, what exactly are you suggesting? You want to move in with me – but not to live as man and wife. You refuse to accept me as a wife accepts her husband?

HELEN: Yes. Why not? Isn't that on?

GEORGE: So why have you come back? Helen!

HELEN: You'd notice the difference soon enough. Believe me, this old bag of bones isn't something you'd even want to touch. Too bad for you. I'm not the same anymore, not the person you see in your mind when you stare at me.

GEORGE: Not the same? Who are you then? Eh? Have you been sealed up? Did that shiny black bastard do it?

HELEN: Don't be vulgar. Calm down. Please calm down.

GEORGE: So you're Helen the mermaid now are you? No, no. You've got two long straight legs, they must lead somewhere.

HELEN: Please keep your hand off me. I'll keep my body covered, buttoned up, if that would make it any easier for you.

GEORGE: You're sick! Sick! You don't belong back in your husband's house. Fine homecoming this turns out to be. You don't belong here – and I won't take you in. Look elsewhere. I won't take you in unless you promise I can *have* you whenever and wherever I want to.

HELEN: I'd mutilate myself, disfigure myself. Do anything to stay with you. Anything, to make you calm again.
(*GEORGE takes her arm and bites deep into it. HELEN pushes her flat hand into his face. He falls over. FIRSTLING and COURTLING jump up to help him.*)

TITANIA: (*Rehearsing, as it were, with OBERON/MIDDLEMASS.*) I know a bank –

OBERON / MIDDLEMASS: I know a bank –

TITANIA: Where the wild thyme –

OBERON / MIDDLEMASS: Where the wild thyme –

TITANIA: Blows!

OBERON / MIDDLEMASS: Blows.

TITANIA: Where oxlips and the nodding violet grows
Quite overcanopied with luscious woodvine
With sweet musk-roses and with eglantine.
You've forgotten it, haven't you?

OBERON / MIDDLEMASS: No…

TITANIA: (*Leans over to him.*) Ah, my Lord. Nothing will come of this. We'll never shed this skin.

OBERON / MIDDLEMASS: I've seen a bank. Where thyme blows. Oxlips. Where, where –

TITANIA: Come along. It's no use. Only a god can save us now.
(*They sit back down at their table.*)

FIRSTLING: (*Referring to OBERON/MIDDLEMASS.*) He's such a nice man.

GEORGE: If anything, too nice. He'd only answer all the junk mail. I'm sorry, we just can't use him, gentlemen.

FIRSTLING: We all know he's lagging behind his true form.

COURTLING: He needs a bit more zip, as they say in football.

FIRSTLING: So do we all. At the end of the day.
(*HELEN, GEORGE, COURTLING exit through curtain.*)
Middlemass. Dickhead. You're causing us no end of problems.
(*He follows the others.*)

HELMA: I think this music's really awful.

WOLF: I just said that. At least you could add 'also', 'I also think this music's really awful.' That's the least you could do. Hey you, what's-yer-name, my co-crashee, show us your sketch!

TITANIA: Leave him alone please.
(*TITANIA and OBERON/MIDDLEMASS exit slowly upstage. WOLF picks up the sketch OBERON/MIDDLEMASS has drawn. Looks at it bewildered.*)

WOLF: Hey, Middlemass. Do you actually know how to drive?

OBERON / MIDDLEMASS: Yes.
(*Slow transformation. The curtain is flown out. In the distance we recognize the following: the BLACK BOY seated at the piano, and various party guests who flit in and out. They are HELEN, GEORGE, WOLF and HELMA. And OBERON. Five of them. A YOUNG WAITER serves drinks. Over the guests' heads, the trapeze occasionally swings to and fro. Empty. Except once. When it has the MAN IN BLACK sitting on it. The hedge now forms the back wall of this tableau. Now and then we hear the last thirty bars or so of Mendelssohn's 'Midsummer Night's Dream Overture'.*)

SCENE 2 – THE TEAR AND THE EAR

Divan, empire style, a formally dressed WAITRESS lolling on it. In front of her, TITANIA's FABLE-SON, whom she is listening to in a dreamy, lascivious way. He hardly seems to notice her. He is on a chair, crossing and uncrossing his legs. He has cattle hoofs instead of feet. Also a little stool further upstage, actually not that little...

SON: We sent out almost fifty invitations, twenty-eight people confirmed. All of five turned up. That'll hurt her. My mother might have hoped that more people would want to celebrate her silver wedding. Was she not popular? Did she not help many people? And now she'll find it difficult to conceal her disappointment and not to make the five people who actually turned up feel that their presence, albeit welcome, is not enough to make her happy. Important though each of them is, they can hardly make up for the missing multitude, the throng required to turn such a day into a true celebration. And even the most important guests will be greeted with a look of unfulfilled anticipation. Which is a shame, because he's here, thank God. And his presence alone is worth more than that of any number of guests, and he personally has given no occasion for disappointment. The finest, the dearest, the single most important guest has arrived, however shrinking, however pitiful his presence may seem compared to the unruly mob of absentees. He was to be the secret trump card, the climax of the evening, but now at best he'll be a small crumb of comfort for her, bearing in mind all those people who didn't come. Now he seems mundane rather than majestic; he cannot stand out from a crowd of lesser guests, for there is no crowd to stand out from. The same will be true, only much, much worse for the second, the third, the fourth most important guests as we go down the social ladder, as it were, and a pathetic ladder it is too, having only five rungs, and the less status each guest has, the more oppressively he will feel the presence of the absent throng, it's unutterable weight forced inexorably down on him by the disappointed face of the hostess whose joyous anniversary this is supposed to be.

(*TITANIA, now old, in a magnificent gown. She peers into the background.*)

TITANIA: One, two, three, four – are the others waiting in the house?

SON: Only *he* is in the house, Mother.

TITANIA: He has come. I've already seen him. He didn't let me down.

SON: You see, my dear, there are exactly five, five wonderful people and we will celebrate with them. No more than five, but also no less. Five people in the park and in the house, all with honest and honourable intentions. Their one dearest wish was to be here with you on this special day.

TITANIA: Five people have come.

How nice. I'm very pleased.

I think I need to fix my hair.

You'll excuse me, little one.

(*She exits.*)

SON: And now, only now, she'll allow herself a few private tears. We should never have planned the festivity on such a grand scale. We should have planned a tiny celebration with an intimate handful of friends – which is actually how it's turned out. We didn't need waiters or cloakroom attendants. Or the caterers or the piano player. We should have kept it intimate. All this grandeur has formed a frost on our tiny circle. And even the most affectionate ambience is somewhat stiffened by serried ranks of superfluous staff. But then – we also thought, well, wasn't this the last opportunity to gather all, or almost all, of her nearest and dearest around her? A lot of people all at once, which of course is the cause of this excess, this extravagance, the joy which one would wish to give to such a mother on such a day. A lot of people all together. A very few people all together. A very few people all together doesn't have quite the same ring to it. It's almost worse than no one at all. She can have that many round for tea on Tuesday. And today's gathering bears no relation to an anniversary party, it's the dullest Tuesday imaginable. A handful of people, like any old week in the year. A little heap of banality. The burnt out embers of dead passions.

89

But no. No – I mustn't make the same mistake I warned my mother about making – getting worked up about the ones who actually came, as opposed to the ones who simply didn't bother. How can the handful help it if they're just a handful? But as for the rest of them –

(*He produces a handkerchief, wipes his mouth, his brow. TITANIA appears with a tea tray.*)

TITANIA: Don't let me disturb you, my boy. I just wanted to have my afternoon tea out here in the sun with you. Just to sniff a bit more sunshine.

SON: Mother – you can't leave your guests waiting.

TITANIA: Of course I can. Today's my party, so I can have my tea alone with you if I want. Today I'll do whatever suits me.

SON: Yes, Mother.

TITANIA: It's right that we should have a moment to ourselves, before we face the hurly-burly, isn't it?

SON: Yes of course.

TITANIA: And it's so lovely to have you to myself for a bit. (*Whispered.*) Haven't you given it a try?

SON: Given what a try? I don't know what you mean.

(*He looks at the WAITRESS on the divan, with an embarrassed smile.*)

TITANIA: My son, oh my son. (*Sighs.*) Everything has its sunny side and its dark side. Life has dealt me so many blows – but it has also provided so many lovely things. And you – you are my greatest joy of all. Goodness gracious. The things you could offer a woman. If only they knew – what sort of man you are. So caring, so clever, so sweet. Men like you don't grow on trees, do they.

SON: No, Mother.

TITANIA: Of course the word hasn't really got round yet. But in our small circle it's Helen Mergentheim who's always speaking fondly of you.

SON: I thought it was Frau Hillewech too.

TITANIA: Yes. Her too. A bit. Sort of. Have you got your eye on her?

SON: I'm only asking. Sometimes you say Frau Hillewech and Frau Mergentheim are tearing each other to bits over me. And now it's just Frau Mergentheim.

TITANIA: Well, all these things change, my child. The mood, the glances, the whole atmosphere. You can't have them both in love with you *every* Tuesday. If you're going to pick one, why not plump for Mergentheim? She's a bit of a religious maniac but her body is faultless.

SON: Mergentheim? I think Hillewech's got a lovely body.

TITANIA: Helma? She's pushing sixty.

SON: What about Helen?

TITANIA: Oh she's a bit younger, a bit younger. Helma, a nice body?… Don't make me laugh! She's a dumpling, a great fat lump.

SON: It's a matter of taste, Mama. I feel that Frau Hillewech has a really attractive figure, whereas I find Frau Mergentheim's beauty rather superficial.

TITANIA: As you wish. If that's your preference then go for Frau Hillewech if anybody.

SON: If anybody… (*He takes her hand, kisses it.*) Mother, I'm so ashamed. So few people have come.

TITANIA: Oh well. It doesn't matter. (*She looks around, wipes away a tear. Gets up.*) So. Got to see to the guests.

SON: You look glorious, Mother. As if it was your wedding day.

TITANIA: You dear boy – you have the craziest notions…!

SON: And now she's clearing the tea things away herself. Just like she does every day. And the little bit which isn't like every day is just like every Tuesday… Dear Lord, why have you not bestowed on us a proper day of celebration? Or one of those bright summer evenings, with a few dozen of your merriest creatures tossed down into our garden by your ever-loving hand, filling it with life and love and acclaim for my dear mother. 'For we will rejoice and we will see, and seeing we will love, and loving we will praise.' Saint Augustine. I had it printed on fifty linen napkins. For whom? For a great bursting banquet, who would not be embarrassed by the exuberance, or the piety of the sentiment. I had it done for a big happy throng, devoted, since time immemorial, to festivity and fun, prepared to enter unabashed into the spirit of the thing. But five friends of the family, looking rather lost? Saint Augustine on their napkins will bring them out in a cold sweat. They'll just be feeling obliged to create such an atmosphere, an atmosphere that even the five oldest and best friends anywhere in the world would be hard pressed to produce. Saint Augustine will bring nothing but sick-making embarrassment. It will have precisely the opposite effect to what was intended. Instead of rejoicing there'll be frost, instead of seeing they'll glance anxiously at each other, instead of loving they'll start bickering. That's how it's going to be, no question. But, whatever you may think of the Five, there's one thing you have to give them credit for: the feeling that this Tuesday should in some way be different from just any old Tuesday in the long history of Tuesdays. On the one hand everyone will be on their guard. On the other they'll be occupying themselves in continual criticism of the absent throng, the very throng in which they hoped to go unnoticed. Me too, I could have done with the throng, I was longing to submerge myself. And then to hunt her down in the throng, to find her hiding, to kiss her and then after supper to lead her back into the throng, standing around in the meadow, drinking wine in the twilight, 'til it's time to go to bed, and I would have put her white Angora jacket round her shoulders and pulled her, still in the throng, pulled her towards me, with the eyes of the throng upon us. All their eyes, all their eyes. Yes it was a clear midsummer's evening. Not a cloud in the sky. The perfect evening for a party. Everyone was beautifully dressed and after supper they all went back into the park, behind the house, and stood around in the twilight, 'til it was time to go to bed. And yes I kissed her, cushioned by the throng. 'This is paradise, my son,' she said. 'Yes,' I said, 'this is paradise, Mother.'

(*The WAITRESS suddenly leaps up in terror.*)

Did you understand all that – or were you just vaguely listening?

Blackout.

SEVEN DOORS

Characters

THE TENANT

THE EXECUTIVE CHAIRMAN

THE FILM DIRECTOR

THE MAN

THE WOMAN

LADY WITH THE MICROPHONE

PROPHET OF DOOM

THE FIRST MAN

THE SECOND MAN

THE SALESMAN

THE CONVICT

THE BODYGUARD

THE SECURITY GUARD

THE MESSENGER

THE SUICIDE

THE VOID

SHE

HE

THE GIRL

THE YOUNG MAN

BROTHER JOHANN

BROTHER FREDDY

COLOMBINE

THE CONTENTED WOMAN

EMPEROR JULIAN

THE QUIET GUY

This translation of *Seven Doors* was first performed on 9 July 2004 at the Chichester Festival Theatre, with the following cast:

THE LANDLORD

THE TENANT, Darlene Johnson
THE CHAIRMAN, Stephen Ventura

COMING HOME

THE FILM DIRECTOR, Chris Jarman
THE MAN, Stephen Ventura
THE WOMAN, Sophie-Louise Dann

AN ERROR

LADY WITH MICROPHONE, Darlene Johnson
PROPHET OF DOOM, Steven Beard

IN THE CAR SHOWROOM

THE FIRST MAN, George Couyas
THE SECOND MAN, Daniel Abelson
THE SALESMAN, Chris Jarman

REFUGE

THE MAN, Stephen Ventura
THE WOMAN, Sophie-Louise Dann
THE CONVICT, Daniel Abelson

THE GUARDS

THE BODYGUARD, Chris Jarman
THE SECURITY GUARD, Steven Beard

THE MESSENGER

THE MESSENGER, Julie Barnes
THE MAN, Stephen Ventura

THE SUICIDE AND THE VOID

THE SUICIDE, Steven Beard
THE VOID, Daniel Abelson

THE EVENING OF THE WEDDING

SHE, Fiona Dunn
HE, George Couyas

IDOLS

THE GIRL, Julie Barnes
THE MAN, Stephen Ventura
THE YOUNG MAN, Daniel Abelson

ON THE LONG BENCH

THE GIRL, Julie Barnes
THE MAN, Stephen Ventura
BROTHER JOHANN, George Couyas
BROTHER FREDDY, Steven Beard
COLOMBINE, Sophie-Louise Dann
THE LADY WITH MICROPHONE, Darlene Johnson
THE CONTENTED WOMAN, Fiona Dunn
EMPEROR JULIAN, Chris Jarman
THE QUIET GUY, Daniel Abelson

Director, Martin Duncan
Designer, Ashley Martin-Davis
Lighting Designer, Sam Gibbons
Sound Designer, Gregory Clarke
Assistant Director, Kieran Hill
Costume Supervisor, Sue Coates
Company Manager, Amelia Ferrand-Rook
Stage Manager, Caroline Healey
Deputy Stage Manager, Kathryn Croft
Assistant Stage Manager, Jo Holt

The scenes are to be played in front of a semi-circle of seven doors, each with translucent glass in its top half.

THE LANDLORD

From two of the doors the EXECUTIVE CHAIRMAN and the TENANT enter.

TENANT: Are you the landlord?

CHAIRMAN: Well, firstly, what's this in connection with?

TENANT: Look, are you or aren't you?

CHAIRMAN: There's a committee which runs this housing association and I am executive chairman of that committee.

TENANT: So, are you my landlord?

CHAIRMAN: Where do you live precisely? Each of our properties has its own administrator, specifically in charge of that particular property.

TENANT: There's no point my talking to middle-men. It's a waste of time.

CHAIRMAN: I do think the best thing is for you to speak to your administrator.

TENANT: You are my landlord, and in your capacity as such I have something to say to you.

CHAIRMAN: I probably won't totally understand what you're talking about. I'm not very well versed in tenancy agreements and the like.

TENANT: Yes, yes, of course. But listen, I live at 15 Otto-Heinrich Street.

CHAIRMAN: So? And? Don't you know who the administrator for that property is?

TENANT: Of course I do.

CHAIRMAN: Then that's the person you need to be talking to.

TENANT: I only want to talk to my landlord.

CHAIRMAN: What particular problem are you having with 15 Otto-Heinrich Street?

TENANT: You're asking me that?

CHAIRMAN: I'm not actually familiar with 15 Otto-Heinrich Street. But I can't be expected to know every single property we own. I'm a management specialist, no more than that.

TENANT: (*Tearing open doors at random.*) Where is my landlord? Show me where he is. I need to talk to the highest authority.

CHAIRMAN: Wait! In our housing association there is no higher authority than myself. So in that respect, you're talking to the right man.

TENANT: Except you don't even know the house I live in.

CHAIRMAN: Well not personally. But obviously I'm aware of it in the abstract, I mean objectively. And a cursory glance at the documents will...

TENANT: So, a man owns a house and doesn't know the house he owns. I've always dreaded that this kind of thing would happen.

CHAIRMAN: How can I make it clear to you that I'm not in any traditional sense a property owner?

TENANT: So, does 15 Otto-Heinrich Street belong to you or not?

CHAIRMAN: Not personally, no.

TENANT: Well what in God's name do you do, personally, then?

CHAIRMAN: Well what I'm doing personally is standing here before you. Which is not to be underestimated. You can't get any higher than me, within the framework of our association.

TENANT: I note your pride, and I note your association, but I'm still lacking a landlord here.

CHAIRMAN: Listen, you're lucky to even be talking to me. You're in at executive level, but that's not enough for you. Oh no. You want to go higher still, to deal with some imaginary Mr Big.

TENANT: I've got something to say to my landlord, that's all.

CHAIRMAN: You know as well as I do that nowadays individual landlords, in the sense you mean, are as rare as hen's teeth.

TENANT: Really? So what do we have in their place?

CHAIRMAN: We have societies, we have trusts, we have consortia and co-operatives, we have wheels within wheels within wheels.

TENANT: Enough of this. These are the fantasies of a lunatic. Paranoid delusions. I want no part of any of it.

CHAIRMAN: I'm sorry but we don't deal with lunacy or with paranoia. We only deal with hard economic facts. And I strongly advise you to relinquish your idealised notion of an individual personalised landlord.

TENANT: He's not an idealised notion. He's a specific person and I need to talk to him. He should, no he must, lend me a sympathetic ear.

CHAIRMAN: So I take it you don't want to talk to me? Someone who can embody the true spirit of the traditional landlord while nevertheless remaining entirely up to date.

TENANT: I don't trust you. And more to the point, you don't even know the house I'm living in. So you're not even aware of my problem. Within my house – and if you were truly my landlord you'd already know this – there is already a house.

CHAIRMAN: What, there's a house inside your house?

TENANT: Absolutely.

CHAIRMAN: What sense am I supposed to make of that?

TENANT: It's not for me to tell you what to think.

CHAIRMAN: Do you by any chance mean that someone is already living there? Another being, another person in your house?

TENANT: No that's not what I mean at all.

CHAIRMAN: No, I suppose not. Because if that were the case, you would have said that there's already a householder inside your house.

TENANT: Exactly.

CHAIRMAN: So what am I supposed to do with that? A house inside a house? Look, I've had a terrible day. A lot of exhausting meetings, loads of stress. And now you cap it all with this.

TENANT: I'm going to say no more about it.

CHAIRMAN: I would prefer that. Because if it were true, we'd have heard about it ages ago. I can assure you this housing association owns no house in which there is already a house. And anyway, get rid of it. Chuck it out. It's a parasite. You don't even need recourse to the process of law. It's the law of the jungle here. Kick it out. Piece of shit!

TENANT: You're so far from being my landlord, I can't begin to tell you. You've convinced me of that if nothing else.

CHAIRMAN: I am your landlord, for crying out loud. And if you don't believe me, I'll make jolly well sure you do. I am the Executive Chairman of this housing association and management company. And as such I have powers. The power to deal with houses and houses that live in houses, and mad bastards who come and tell me about houses living in houses, exactly as I wish. Of that you can be sure.

TENANT: Since I have decided to say no more about it and shortly to leave the tricky situation I have described to you in your not so capable hands, I can assure you that you'll soon discover that your powers, as you call them, certainly vis-à-vis the house at 15 Otto-Heinrich St, will turn out to be distinctly limited.

CHAIRMAN: All right, look, fine. Let's both of us keep our hair on and be civil about this. 'Nice and easy does it every time.' Okay, how long has there been a house living in your…oh for *fuck's sake*. What am I doing even saying this nonsense? If I say it, I might end up believing it. That'll be next. I promise I'm being as nice to you as I can, but there are limits my friend, there are limits.

TENANT: You're only getting angry with yourself.

CHAIRMAN: No, I'm getting angry with you. You're making my brain ache. What you're telling me is poison, pure poison.

TENANT: Well, why did you engage me in conversation in the first place when you're quite palpably and demonstrably not my landlord?

CHAIRMAN: I am, I am, I am. Be quiet.

TENANT: No, no. You're the one who should have been quiet. You would have been much better advised to do nothing rather than open this whole can of worms.

CHAIRMAN: But you were threatening me from the minute I came out of the committee room. Threatening me with your dangerous nonsense, with your whole mad whirling being. You must know better than most how hard it is to get rid of a raving lunatic.

TENANT: You're right, it's tricky.

CHAIRMAN: People like that, it's as if they inject you with their insanity. And then there's nothing you can do about it. You have to wait till the stuff's been twice round your system and starts to wear off. Same thing happened to me in the board room, when Mr Schimmelpfennig had his nervous breakdown. As a result of which he withdrew his candidature for the committee. He was totally overworked, totally stressed out, and he started to crack up. And I tell you, from then on in, I thought I was going to crack up too. Everything became too much for me. The filing cabinets became a grey wall. The room became a rubber cell. And I thought to myself, one more mad word from anybody and I tell you I'm going over the edge.

TENANT: I came here in search of my landlord and I find a Executive Chairman on the verge of a nervous breakdown. What a waste of my valuable time.

CHAIRMAN: You've going to have to believe me. I'm not normally a bundle of nerves.

TENANT: You were born a bundle of nerves, and since your birth you've never been anything but a bundle of nerves.

CHAIRMAN: You're mistaken.

TENANT: I'm absolutely not mistaken.

CHAIRMAN: If only you knew the razor sharp accuracy with which I conduct my daily business affairs.

TENANT: Be that as it may, I can spot a bundle of nerves at a cursory glance. I could spot one a hundred metres away. I can go up to a bundle of nerves and name it. I can say, this is what you are. I have an infallible instinct.

CHAIRMAN: You plainly haven't.

TENANT: I certainly have.

CHAIRMAN: Yeah whatever.

TENANT: Ha! (*In the sense of 'you listen to me'.*)

CHAIRMAN: Yeah. (*In the sense of 'I tell it like it is'.*)

TENANT: Tss! (*In the sense of 'he doesn't believe me'.*)

(*There follow an exchange of noises as each protagonist maintains his position in the argument.*)

CHAIRMAN: Pffff!

TENANT: Hm! (*An amused falsetto.*)

CHAIRMAN: Phhh!

TENANT: Bbbbb. (*Blowing a raspberry.*)

CHAIRMAN: Kkkk. (*Like hissy white noise.*)

TENANT: A. (*Short, dismissive.*)

CHAIRMAN: Mm. (*Hummed slightly thoughtfully.*)

TENANT: Mm. (*Also hummed, also slightly thoughtfully.*)

(*Enter through one of the doors the FILM DIRECTOR and the WOMAN.*)

COMING HOME

FILM DIRECTOR: Okay. Here's the TV, underneath it's the
    video. Okay? You're watching the very end of the show,
    watching the final minutes of *Name That Tune.* Your
    husband's sitting there in the glass box up on the stage
    and Thomas Schwarze is about to ask him the very last
    question.

(*The translucent glass in one of the doors becomes clear, and we
see the top half of the MAN wearing headphones.*)

And everything, but everything, is hanging on this one
question. It's all or nothing. And he's sweating, he's chewing
his lower lip. And then it comes, 'Name That Tune'. He
hears the first few bars, and suddenly like a pistol shot he
answers. And equally suddenly there's a great big shout,
from you, from the watching millions, from one enormous
throat… 'Wrong!' Wrong answer. Game over. He's lost.
Everything. You stand up, you go over to the sideboard,
and you take a good healthy swig from the whisky bottle.
In the actual movie, I'll be cutting away to the streets of the
town; they'll all be empty, not a soul there. Everyone will be
sitting in front of their tellies, nervously shovelling peanuts
into their mouths, and then suddenly one great shout will
echo through the streets, coming from all the windows
at once. Meanwhile, you'll be at home alone, and you'll
wander aimlessly through the apartment, putting everything
that's already in place even more firmly and finally in place.
In the end, you'll go up to a long-stemmed vase, you'll
hesitate for a second, and then smash it into smithereens
with a single karate chop. You'll have recorded the show
on video, so you play the moment of defeat over and over
again. You murmur to yourself, 'I bet he doesn't call.'
Cut to the next scene, the return of the defeated contestant.
He comes in, sits silently at the dinner table, and begins to
eat, mindlessly, mechanically.

(*The MAN comes to one of the doors, sits at the table and begins
to eat. The DIRECTOR withdraws.*)

MAN: So. Did you get a look at our Far Eastern friend?

WOMAN: Oh you mean the winner?

MAN: Jumped up little prick.

WOMAN: He knew his stuff, he won fair and square.

MAN: Smart alecky cheeky little chink. Some know-it-all bit part player in some Chinese operetta. He impressed you did he? I tell you one thing, that Thomas Schwarze is the most ignorant bastard I've even had the misfortune to meet. If he didn't have the answers on his little bits of card…

WOMAN: Horst, you know absolutely nothing.

MAN: I knew it wasn't Liszt.

WOMAN: Of course it wasn't, it was *Tristan and Isolde.*

MAN: I know. But I'm more of a Liszt expert.

WOMAN: Okay but you must have been able to hear that it wasn't *Hansel and Gretel.* What have we been swotting for, for months on end? Day after day. Even at night, with the cassette recorder under the pillow. What was it all for?

MAN: Oh come on. It's just a game. It's only a game.

WOMAN: What on earth made you think it was Humperdinck?

MAN: Don't ask me. Don't ever ask me anything again.

WOMAN: We've never even listened to any Humperdinck.

MAN: Maybe you haven't. I have. And anyway the whole thing goes much further back than you think. My first piano teacher, back in the beginning of the fifties, was a communist.

WOMAN: Go into your office. Concentrate on your databanks. Leave knowledge well alone.

MAN: You're right. Draw a veil over the whole thing. There are more important things in life than Liszt and co.

WOMAN: Actually, the more I think of it, there's nothing more important in life than the fact that you gave the wrong answer.

MAN: Ah well. Come tomorrow it'll all look different.

WOMAN: I've a horrible feeling that come tomorrow it'll all look the same.

MAN: Really? Do you think so? Well anyway…the smart thing is to concede.

WOMAN: No, I don't think so. I think the smart thing is to keep winning.

MAN: Yep. You're going to be doomed to spend the rest of
your life saddled with a quiz show loser.
(*From one of the doors come the LADY WITH THE MICROPHONE
and the PROPHET OF DOOM. They sit on a sofa.*)

AN ERROR

LADY WITH THE MICROPHONE: Mr Gorschinski, for over twenty years now your published works have been warning us about mankind's capacity for self-destruction.

PROPHET OF DOOM: What? I'm terribly sorry I don't hear awfully well…

LADY WITH THE MICROPHONE: (*Louder.*) For over twenty years you've… No that's too loud. If I shout like that, with the microphone, it'll distort the sound. Do you understand what I'm saying?

PROPHET OF DOOM: Ah well, you see, none of this is in fact so terribly new. It must be over twenty years ago that I contended in one of my books that our destiny as a species, mankind that is, the so-called pinnacle of all creation, is looking distinctly dubious. And today, I would go as far as to say…

LADY WITH THE MICROPHONE: (*Repeating her intro at medium volume.*) Mr Gorschinski,

PROPHET OF DOOM: Hello?

LADY WITH THE MICROPHONE: …For over twenty years now your published works have been warning us about mankind's capacity for self-destruction. (*She masks the microphone.*) Do you understand what I'm saying?

PROPHET OF DOOM: That is correct.

LADY WITH THE MICROPHONE: Good. Would you contend that in the intervening years, events have substantiated your theories?

PROPHET OF DOOM: I say, could you possibly speak a little louder?

LADY WITH THE MICROPHONE: I was wondering if you believed that your theories… No stop. Once more from the top. I need the right question. Otherwise we won't be able to edit.

PROPHET OF DOOM: Well you see, the history of mankind, the historical envelope if you will, contains merely six thousand years or so. Comparatively speaking, we are still young.

LADY WITH THE MICROPHONE: (*Loudly.*) Could you just hang on a second? Wait for the question. I have to ask the question first.

PROPHET OF DOOM: I'd have to say yes. Sadly yes, but yes nonetheless. Without a shadow of doubt. You could take any one of my books and triply underline any sentence therein, and still not come anywhere near the reality of the disastrous developments of the last decade.

LADY WITH THE MICROPHONE: Do you mean that you stick by your contention that man is some sort of technical error in the programming of all creation?

PROPHET OF DOOM: An error? Oh dear me. I wonder what you're referring to. Of course it's entirely possible in a work of this magnitude that some tiny slip of the pen might have occurred. I suspect that it's to a certain extent unavoidable. But which specific passage are you referring to?

LADY WITH THE MICROPHONE: No, nothing specific, I meant just in general. If I understand you correctly, you're saying that mankind is, in and of itself, an error. (*Louder.*) Mankind as error.

PROPHET OF DOOM: Oh yes, absolutely of course. Now I see what you're saying. I'm sorry, for a moment there I was miles away. Where were we? Oh yes, an error. I'd go further than that. The error. Absolutely. Definitely. Mankind, nature's mistake. The human brain an evolutionary blind alley. You can look at it that way, and indeed I have looked at it that way. It seems to me self-evident.

LADY WITH THE MICROPHONE: But in spite of everything, do you not retain the slightest glint of optimism?

PROPHET OF DOOM: And I'd like to add, if I may, that I'll always look at it that way in the future. Should I be given the opportunity of actually having a future. (*He laughs.*)

IN THE CAR SHOWROOM

Two MEN and a young SALESMAN sitting on the couch. A perspex column displays the latest models.

FIRST MAN: Has there been a road test on the tyres of this model?

(The SALESMAN suddenly lurches and doubles up with his head on his knees.)

Every time I ask you a question you double up.

(Both men put him back in position.)

SECOND MAN: So, anyway. What's new.

FIRST MAN: I get the feeling you're no stranger to insanity.

SECOND MAN: You're not really up to us, are you?

FIRST MAN: Customers like us, with our philosophical tendencies…got to be your idea of a nightmare.

SECOND MAN: But even when we're dealing with a car in this price bracket, the Socrates in us both cannot be kept in check. Gradually we start to question the nature of the thing. The object.

FIRST MAN: And we are increasingly convinced that this car could fill a car-shaped gap in us.

SECOND MAN: But whether it's in good enough nick can only be ascertained by road testing a hitherto un-roadtested example of this and no other model.

FIRST MAN: We wish to introduce into the traffic arena a hitherto untested, untouched, unadulterated automobile.

SECOND MAN: A colt of a car. Young, skittish, frisky, yet wilful.

FIRST MAN: We are not a common occurrence on the forecourt. Car lovers who are, what?

SECOND MAN: Thinkers.

FIRST MAN: Absolutely.

SECOND MAN: Philosophers.

FIRST MAN: Indeed. Not something you meet every day.

SECOND MAN: Not every day.

FIRST MAN: Wife? Kid? Kids?

(The SALESMAN nods and then collapses again. The two MEN push him back into position.)

SECOND MAN: Daughter where?

SALESMAN: Abroad.

FIRST MAN: Aha.

SECOND MAN: Weak dollar.

FIRST MAN: No way.

SECOND MAN: No?

FIRST MAN: Not for years.

SALESMAN: Why car?

FIRST MAN: Like we said, fill a gap.

SECOND MAN: With a dream machine.

FIRST MAN: What I've always imagined is a car shaped like something that swallowed itself. But I look around and sadly see nothing of the sort on display.

SALESMAN: How come you take the liberty of thinking that we don't stock such a…

FIRST MAN: What do you mean take liberties? I wouldn't dream of taking liberties with you.

SALESMAN: No I meant, taking the liberty of something as opposed to taking liberties with someone.

SECOND MAN: You may have meant the one but you said the other.

FIRST MAN: You certainly said the other, though you may have meant the one.

SECOND MAN: You meant the one and said the other. Or one or the other.

FIRST MAN: In any case, what's clear is that it's an insult, the sort of insult there's no way of wriggling your way out of.

SALESMAN: Please God, let me never ever understand what you're on about.

FIRST MAN: Little chance of that, little chance of that.

SECOND MAN: Do your damnedest, do your damnedest.

SALESMAN: I can't stand this. I can't stand this. (*He runs off behind the door.*)

FIRST MAN: An endless afternoon of miserable moments stretches before us.

SECOND MAN: Nothing and no one to attach ourselves to.

FIRST MAN: Car salesmen these days need nerves of steel.

SECOND MAN: They have to be like coppersmiths.

FIRST MAN: But nonetheless, move with the times.

SECOND MAN: But only for a while and then it's back into the garden of earthly delights. Gorgeous!

FIRST MAN: As naked as Jupiter, bereft of poetry.

SECOND MAN: As nude as a poodle.

FIRST MAN: As nude as a poodle's noodle.

SECOND MAN: As oodles of poodle's noodles.

FIRST MAN: Absolutely.

(*SALESMAN reappears from behind one of the doors.*)

SECOND MAN: Just now you were dangerously near to insanity again.

SALESMAN: I've turned the satellite navigation system on.

SECOND MAN: Just now we were the unwitting cause in you of a state of excitement which the outside observer would doubtless typify as excessive, but now, you seem to be claiming the complete opposite.

FIRST MAN: If you've ever been able to imagine what it must be like to have the celebrated sword of Damocles hanging over you, then you'll have a rough idea of how it must feel to spend your meagre existence beneath the transmitting arm of a TV satellite.

SECOND MAN: Which covers from Copenhagen to Trieste.

FIRST MAN: But put yourself in the shoes of someone who needs a car to take him either up beyond Copenhagen or down past Trieste.

SALESMAN: Now, let me tell you how the starter works.

FIRST MAN: The starter? What do you mean by that?

SALESMAN: The thing that starts the thing.

SECOND MAN: The thing that started all known things?

FIRST MAN: Again he drives us back into the metaphysical. Like a shepherd with his lambs.

SECOND MAN: Like a lamb-loving muttonhead.

FIRST MAN: Like a mutton-headed cowherd.

SECOND MAN: Like a cow-eyed pigherd.

FIRST MAN: Like a pig-bellied oxherd.

SECOND MAN: Like an ox-tailed goatherd.

SALESMAN: You're somnambulists. Somnambulists.

FIRST MAN: Your favourite word. His favourite word.

SECOND MAN: Very cool, very detached.

FIRST MAN: Not my style at all.

SECOND MAN: If you've had enough of us just say the word and we'll take the matter up with your immediate superiors.

FIRST MAN: One thing however you should have no illusions about, we're not going to set foot outside this showroom without a car.

SECOND MAN: And a gorgeous car to boot.

FIRST MAN: Absolutely. You should find that condition somewhat liberating. Which doesn't make the matter any easier. Merely more unprecedented.

REFUGE

On the couch the MAN and the WOMAN.

MAN: Your mother, who now seems to be lodging with us, with a convict in tow, a man whom she was at first taking care of, and who has now become her lover…this respectable wife of a Lutheran minister from Neckarsulm who has been taking refuge with us for a week now…all I want to do is get to know her. A bit. Just the chance to say hello would be nice.

WOMAN: I don't know if she wants to see anybody. She's much too much in love.

MAN: But she's living here in our apartment. She's supposed to be our guest. To want to see her face is surely not too much to ask.

WOMAN: She never leaves her room. She spends all day in bed with him.

MAN: Tell me what actually happened.

WOMAN: It all started when he was in jail and they began to exchange letters. At first they were decent and God-fearing, then they became more and more affectionate, and now it's progressed to pure passion.

MAN: That's taking reintegration into society a touch too far, don't you think. Does your father know?

WOMAN: Yes, he knows. He doesn't know they're here. But he knows they ran away together.

MAN: Aren't you just a little bit embarrassed, I mean deep down?

WOMAN: Embarrassed? (*She laughs.*) No, why should I be? I'm thrilled my mother's so happy.

MAN: What about your father, aren't you sorry for him?

WOMAN: It's his own fault. If he hadn't poisoned us all with his vile odour of sanctity none of this would ever have happened.

MAN: I don't agree. Things like this don't have causes. They merely occur. For no reason. And the husband, poor old bloke, has to suffer. That's the way it is.

WOMAN: You don't know him. He's like Job, but a good deal
more garrulous. He talks his way through his misery.

MAN: You're a good decent woman. Wipe that demonic smile
off your face.

(*The CONVICT, a frail man with wild unkempt hair, enters from
one of the seven doors. He is wrapped in a large towel.*)

CONVICT: Did I hear someone mention Job? If so, you won't
mind if I oblige you with a small quotation, 'I desire you to
listen to me, not to tempt me with false comforters.' Believe
me, I've shouted those words a thousand times, more, in
my prison cell.

(*The CONVICT sits between them on the couch.*)

You remember that ferry disaster in the channel? Well the
man who declared himself guilty straight away, admitting
he'd neglected to shut the dock doors immediately after
the ship had set sail, and as a result, allowed tons of water
to pour into the ferry and completely scupper it within
a matter of minutes… That man wanted, needed, to be
the guilty party. But the authorities wouldn't allow it.
The legal authorities, the shipping company, the freight
line, all stood up against him. He couldn't be guilty they
said, incomprehensible. Just him? But it was just him. His
negligence had caused the death of 135 people, how can
he possibly atone for all that? But he wanted to. He wanted
to carry the massive burden of repentance on his own
shoulders. You have to admit, that it's a pretty poor reason
to commit a crime; doing it merely to come in contact
with the full force of the punishment meted out by the law,
and I doubt if such a person still exists. Most of them are
rough godless creatures, seemingly committed to reducing
or even ending their sentences, but in reality, only wishing
to get out of jail in order to commit fresh crimes, great
or small. And eventually I suppose, to come in contact
again with the full force of the punishment meted out by
the law. I doubt if you'd catch anyone doing it nowadays.
Most prisoners are rough, godless creatures. I tell you
this…a criminal, in his deepest heart and his darkest soul,
is merely a penitent monk, a flagellant, a masochist for

115

Christ. He is not a victim of society, nor of his background, he is an addict. He is hooked on punishment. What am I talking about?

(*He strikes his skull with both fists and then holds them in front of his face.*)

My bloody mind! It's got nothing to do with the two of us has it? There's something rotten in my mind, in my miserable mind. And it's got nothing to do with 'us'.

MAN: (*To WOMAN.*) What did he actually do?

CONVICT: (*Stands up suddenly.*) I think I'd much rather not be here.

(*Behind one of the doors we hear a female VOICE.*)

VOICE: Mischa, Mischa…

CONVICT: And if people want to start talking about me this is all you need to know. I'm off. (*He exits through the door.*)

MAN: He was totally in the grip of anger.

WOMAN: When his face goes red you can see prison bars carved in his forehead.

(*Behind the doors you can hear the sounds of cars in a parking garage. Enter the BODYGUARD and the SECURITY GUARD.*)

THE GUARDS

BODYGUARD: Were you looking for a bodyguard?

SECURITY GUARD: Yes.

BODYGUARD: Just for yourself?

SECURITY GUARD: Yes.

BODYGUARD: Can I ask what you do for a living?

SECURITY GUARD: I'm a security guard. I'm in charge of this entire multi-storey car park.

BODYGUARD: So you're a security guard for a car park?

SECURITY GUARD: That's it.

BODYGUARD: And you're looking for someone, is this right, to guard you while you're guarding the cars?

SECURITY GUARD: Not just that. I'm looking for someone to accompany me from my home to my work in the mornings and then back again in the evenings. Furthermore, I would require him to stand guard outside where I'm living in at the moment.

BODYGUARD: My dear chap, have you any idea what that costs?

SECURITY GUARD: I can imagine. I've asked around.

BODYGUARD: You've asked around. So what you seem to be looking for is a full round-the-clock service. Is your life in any particular danger at the moment?

SECURITY GUARD: There's always danger.

BODYGUARD: Well obviously, that goes without saying. I mean you could be attacked. The car park could be robbed and razed to the ground.

SECURITY GUARD: Exactly. And that's just one example.

BODYGUARD: Excuse me, but by the same token, everyone needs a personal bodyguard. And before long, every slightly weaker person will have signed up his slightly stronger friend for his personal protection.

SECURITY GUARD: Which in my opinion would be totally socially appropriate.

BODYGUARD: In which case, I would be obliged to take on someone slightly stronger than myself as my bodyguard and he would have to find someone slightly stronger in turn. My God, our entire society would consist of an endless conga-chain of personal security staff.

SECURITY GUARD: And at the end of the chain, at the end of it, logically speaking, would be the strongest man of all.

BODYGUARD: Correct.

SECURITY GUARD: And then we'd know who he was. We'd have found out who the strongest man in the world actually was, but in the most natural and socially acceptable way imaginable.

BODYGUARD: Stop talking. This is nonsense.

SECURITY GUARD: Imaginable but in the last analysis impracticable. It would mean, if one is to demand absolute fairness and consistency, that I would have to be at the end of the chain because I can only look after cars. I can't look after people. There could be no one below me. All that there could be below me would be the world of empty cars in a multi-storey car park.

BODYGUARD: Okay, to cut to the chase, twenty-four hour personal protection that would come to several thousand marks a month. Considerably more than twice what you earn. And on top of that, I would be an employee, so you've got to add health benefits, national insurance, pension schemes…the lot. We do live in a civilised country.

SECURITY GUARD: None of that should be an obstacle. I promise you you won't want for anything. I'll share my salary with you.

BODYGUARD: Your salary? Which is what? Two thousand net?

SECURITY GUARD: Two thousand five hundred.

BODYGUARD: Look, I'm only listening to you out of sympathy. What I should be doing is demanding my travel expenses and making you regret that you were impertinent enough to ask me to come here in the first place. I'm only listening to you because I find you amusing, and because I feel sorry for you.

SECURITY GUARD: The fact you're sympathetic is a good sign. I mean without that this isn't going to work at all. I took on this dreadful menial job after the sudden death of my brother. There was no punishment. No laws, no courts forcing me to do penance. And even if the case had gone before God Almighty, my ramshackle life would have been completely unaffected. I would have carried on as before. If I hadn't brought all this on myself, if I hadn't punished myself by taking on this undignified work with parked cars, trust me nothing would have happened to me, nothing at all. No penance would have been demanded of me. In the old days it was sackcloth and ashes. Nowadays it's exhaust fumes.

BODYGUARD: By the sound of it, you're bearing the burden of guilt for your brother's death.

SECURITY GUARD: You're right, that's exactly what I'm doing. I knew he was going to die, I knew it precisely. And I never told him.

BODYGUARD: I doubt if he would have been very keen to hear it.

SECURITY GUARD: No, that's where you're wrong. You obviously don't know my brother. He wanted to know everything ahead of time, as precisely as he could, down to the minutest detail, and to adjust his behaviour accordingly. He was pedantic to a fault.

BODYGUARD: But he himself didn't notice that he was dying, or doomed to die, or about to die or whatever?

SECURITY GUARD: No, he didn't notice a thing I promise you. Not a blessed thing. He stood here inside the kiosk and death came and took him. He touched an exposed cable with a drop of coffee still on his finger and there he was, dead.

BODYGUARD: But how could you possibly know ahead of time that such a random sort of accident was going to happen to him?

SECURITY GUARD: Because he always reads everything. It was a compulsion with him, to read everything he saw. I'd made a little notice for him, a tiny piece of paper with the words 'Danger! Do Not Touch!' written on it in tiny tiny script. I attached a strip of sellotape to it and sort of blew it upwards, let it kind of flutter upwards towards where the newly installed cable was hidden behind the fuse-box. And I thought to myself, 'It's okay, he will read it, he will read it.'

BODYGUARD: In that case you sent the man to his death! Or to be more precise, let me take this slowly... In the first place, you must take a share in the responsibility for your own brother's death. Obviously the main burden of guilt must lie with the building supervisors, who had no business leaving live cables lying around.

SECURITY GUARD: Obviously. We know that. But my crime can't be that I didn't warn him that there was the possibility of his dying, after all I did write 'Danger! Do Not Touch'. No, my crime can only have been that I knew that he would die and didn't tell him.

BODYGUARD: Maybe instead of writing in miniscule script on a tiny Post-It note, you might have been better off hanging up a huge piece of cardboard with a large skull and crossbones painted on it.

SECURITY GUARD: The trouble is he never understood those sort of symbols. We were always squabbling about it. He could never decipher them. He was always going in to the wrong toilet, that whole Ladies, Gents, pictogram thing, he could never make head nor tail of it. Traffic symbols? A real problem. He was visually handicapped vis-à-vis symbols. Letters, letters, letters, that's what he wanted. He devoured them. And, oddly enough, the smaller the better. Words for him had to be tiny, tidgy, teeny-weeny, teensy-weensy, otherwise he wouldn't give them the time of day. Like I said, he was a pedant. If he'd seen a skull and crossbones he would have assumed it meant 'Beware of the Dog' and torn it down. He would have thought someone was taking the piss, and fair enough. He'd never have known that there was any danger.

BODYGUARD: Well, assuming that the sequence of events was exactly as you described...secondly, and secondly is a question... I have to know *why* in God's name – and if I don't get a satisfactory answer to this question that means you've been leading me up the garden path, in which case in the name of all that's sacred I will demonstrate to you precisely what doing penance actually feels like, and I promise you that 'Danger! Do Not Touch' doesn't come close to it: so take my advice, don't lead me into another conversational thicket and just dump me there – again I have to ask *why* in God's name would your stupid brother have been happy – *happy!* – if he'd known that he was dying or about to die?

SECURITY GUARD: Because…there was for him no greater pleasure in life than knowing that he was plunging me into deep despair, and his death plunged me into deep despair straight away. But now I've punished, humiliated and abased myself so much and for so long I've become quite debilitated. Which is why I feel I've now earned the right for protection.

BODYGUARD: You should get God Almighty to be your bodyguard. He comes for free.

SECURITY GUARD: You're stronger than he is. You understand the obligations of brotherhood, although I would appreciate it if you'd refrain from light-hearted blasphemy.

BODYGUARD: To cut a long story short, you're begging me, aren't you?

SECURITY GUARD: I don't deny it. I am poor in strength, whereas you are rich. I'm downtrodden, whereas you are fearless. It's only natural that such contradictory characteristics should seek to complement each other. You receive, by dint of my weakness, an undeniable corroboration of your strength. And that is the strength I need.

BODYGUARD: Listen. I've protected managing directors, barmaids, politicians and Robert Lembke, the quiz show host. Each of these individuals had to find some way of enticing me to be their personal security advisor.

SECURITY GUARD: I don't want to blow my own trumpet, but I do think that I could become one of those individuals. I think I could entice you.

BODYGUARD: You're a hobgoblin, that's what you are. Alright then, tell me what you're so afraid of.

SECURITY GUARD: I'm afraid of every form of violence which I could potentially protect myself against. To put it more precisely, I'm not afraid of atom bombs, population explosions, meteors, epidemics, or any acts of God or of fate. But I am afraid of, I'll give you an example, a shoot-out in my immediate vicinity.

BODYGUARD: That's still not something that happens every day.

SECURITY GUARD: Well, the worst thing that could possibly happen, by definition only ever happens once. But when it does, that's when you really want to have a bodyguard.

BODYGUARD: Be that as it may, all you seem to have is a childish need to hide behind your big brother. You're obviously missing him, that's all.

SECURITY GUARD: No, no. He was actually my little brother. That's the most depressing thing about the whole story. He was always the little guy who worked in the car park. And then in my agony and despair I rushed aimlessly to and fro before finally deciding to take his place.

BODYGUARD: And now you're seriously suggesting that for half your salary I should…

SECURITY GUARD: You can share my flat as well.

BODYGUARD: …I should stand here next to you, in the exhaust fumes, and completely poison my lungs.

SECURITY GUARD: Think of the massive personal security that you yourself would gain. If you were protecting some high-up politician then you'd have to be dealing with assassins twenty-four-seven. So at every second your life could be in danger. At your age, you'd maybe want to think twice before throwing yourself in front of some member of parliament, probably not a particularly popular one, and ending your days in a hail of bullets. If you spend your time with me, an ordinary man, a man of the people, surely the risk of coming face to face with a would-be assassin is considerably reduced. Being with a man like me guarantees you a professional survival rate of eighty, ninety, no ninety-five per cent. Which is a serious consideration not to be ignored. On the one hand the almost unavoidable hail of bullets, on the other a five per cent risk of dying on the job. And that five per cent already includes lung damage through exhaust fume inhalation, and any other unforeseen dramas.

BODYGUARD: How can I put this more clearly? You don't need a bodyguard. No one's going to do anything to you. A poor sad frog like you. Just behave properly, keep your nose clean and nothing will happen.

SECURITY GUARD: So, I'm a poor sad frog, am I? So what if I am? If that's how I appear to you, then okay. Fair enough. But I'm sure you'll remember that in the fairy tale the frog who gets smashed against a wall turns into a handsome prince.

BODYGUARD: So you want me to smash you against the wall?

SECURITY GUARD: You don't have to go that far. All I need you to do is to sign a deal with me. And then you'll find out who I've got behind me.

BODYGUARD: So some kind of rich uncle from America type thing?

SECURITY GUARD: That I'm not at liberty to divulge. But I should tell you you're on the right track.

BODYGUARD: Do you know who's behind you? I do. A whole international organisation of poor sad frogs like you. An endless queue of weeds and weaklings, that's who I see behind you. You're not the guy who dares to stand alone, I spotted that straight away. But I'm not going to play the Stupid Giant for some posse of bed-wetters and wimps. I'm not a giant and I'm certainly not a Good Samaritan. I'm a salaried employee who happens to have broad shoulders and is trained in the use of firearms. I offer a security service to VIPs. I don't protect parking attendants. That not what I do, that's not what my training was devised for. Even if thirty dwarfs were to offer me a thousand marks a month, each, to stand guard outside their cave, I wouldn't guard a single one of them. I don't guard dwarfs. If you're small, fine, you club together and look after yourselves. If you're big, and if you stand alone, then you stick out, and that's when you need my protection.

SECURITY GUARD: That's the sort of moral stance you'll have to adopt less and less when you're my bodyguard.

BODYGUARD: I will never be your bodyguard. Never, do you hear? Never!

SECURITY GUARD: Well that's the half an hour trial period over with, and…congratulations, you've done it! The job's yours! God, what a relief! No, really, I'm delighted with you. Just the ticket. A stimulating conversation is maybe the best protection a man can enjoy… Look! Over there!

BODYGUARD: Oh my God, what is that? A monster. An ogre.

SECURITY GUARD: Yes a real giant! Look at him… No, no, don't shoot! Look, he's going of his own accord. He had no choice. His time was up. And he didn't get me!

(*All the doors open at once. Office sounds. Telephones, computers, printers. From door to door EMPLOYEES pass, carrying documents and folders. From upstage we hear someone carrying a heavy weight. The MAN is alone on stage. Through one door, the MESSENGER arrives, carrying a large package.*)

THE MESSENGER

MESSENGER: Mr Horst Tietze.

MAN: That's me.

MESSENGER: I've brought the special package.

MAN: For me? I knew it! Heavy package isn't it?

MESSENGER: Yes. Heavy with import, one might say.

   (*The MESSENGER writes in an order book.*)

   And what do you do, Mr Tietze? Professionally, I mean.

MAN: My profession? Oh, you know, something or other.

MESSENGER: You don't have a profession?

MAN: Oh yes I do, absolutely. What was it again? Hang on a
   second, I wrote it down somewhere…

MESSENGER: Don't worry. It's not essential.

MAN: All professions look so alike nowadays. Everyone
   collecting and hoarding data. Looking at their fluorescent
   screens, scrabbling around for what they can earn, and
   put by. That's all there is to it when all's said and done.
   (*He looks at the package.*) So you've got everything in here
   needed for multilateral world-wide disarmament?

MESSENGER: This package contains the most vital instruments
   appertaining to both world powers. Without them nothing
   will work any more. Now they're in your hands.

MAN: Why me of all people?

MESSENGER: Your address was picked from over a million
   candidates as belonging to one of the most insignificant
   men in the entire world.

MAN: How could you possibly know that I'm one of the most
   insignificant men in the world?

MESSENGER: With the help of modern technology a man such
   as yourself can be selected from the world's population in
   less than half a second.

MAN: I can imagine. And I do recognise the irony of
   my situation. I seem to have come first in the World
   Insignificance Championships. Which has, by definition, to
   signify something.

MESSENGER: Come what may, your anonymity will be
   preserved. Apart from myself, only the Programme
   knows your true identity, and the whereabouts of the

Disarmament Package. And I personally am under strictest instructions from the Programme that I can only pass on your name and address in the most extreme circumstances.

MAN: What am I supposed to do with the package?

MESSENGER: Don't open it, and put it in the wardrobe in your bedroom. Within a certain, and as yet unspecified period of time, it will be picked up and sent on somewhere else.

MAN: Where?

MESSENGER: From one person to the next.

MAN: So it all stays secret?

MESSENGER: Secret? Well that depends what you mean by secret. Let's say anonymous. At least as anonymous as you or I…

THE SUICIDE AND THE VOID

Empty stage. The SUICIDE and the VOID stand opposite each other.

SUICIDE: So you're the Void then?

VOID: You must be the Suicide. Hi.

SUICIDE: You're the Void?

VOID: Yep.

> (*The SUICIDE bursts out laughing. The VOID has no choice but to
> join in. The SUICIDE slaps the VOID on the shoulders.*)

SUICIDE: (*Sarcastically.*) Oh yes, that's exactly how I imagined
the Void would be! Just this ordinary bloke.

VOID: Sorry to disappoint you.

SUICIDE: I mean come on, we're talking about the void here,
the eternal nothingness, I mean at least you could have
been something…something awe-inspiring, something
inconceivable. And not just…

VOID: Look, I think we can spare ourselves half an hour of
sniffing around each other, if that's okay with you?

SUICIDE: But, just an average sort of meeting, just bumping
into this bloke, like 'oh hi'! I hadn't reckoned on that. And
here I am stuck with you for all eternity.

VOID: Well yes, you have passed beyond.

SUICIDE: Yes. I'm all too aware of that. That I've passed
beyond. There's no going back now. No point in even
trying. And no hope, I'm assuming, of some sort of early
separation? No?

VOID: No. I'm your void and so I will remain.

SUICIDE: I think you might well drive me to despair.

VOID: We both have to be prepared for that eventuality.

SUICIDE: Look. How, in the name of all that's holy, is it
possible that someone like myself, who has had the
courage to take his own life and in the process has touched
upon, if I say it myself, tragic greatness, can be now be
lumbered with this, this nobody, who claims to be The
Void, but in his stature and demeanour will for all eternity
remind me inexorably of no one else but my rather sweaty
lab assistant Hugenstock!? I mean there must be more to a
Void than that!

VOID: I tell what you want to do. You see me as grey on grey…you want to try painting me more in primary colours, fiery red, that kind of thing. And you'd do well to think of what you plainly see as my complete ordinariness as some sort of punishment meant only for you.

SUICIDE: In other words: the fact that I'm destined to be inescapably and ineluctably bored and irritated by you for ever and ever amen, should merely be looked at as my personal purgatory?

VOID: (*Giggles.*) Your whatty whatty?

SUICIDE: My personal purgatory. And stop being childish.

VOID: Sorry. It just sounded funny, that's all. Sorry, I'll try and stop laughing. Promise you won't start? (*Struggles with the giggles.*)

SUICIDE: I was just asking you if my being stuck with you, boring ordinary prat that you are, is my personal purgatory.

VOID: (*Howls with laughter again.*) Stop it!

SUICIDE: My limbo, my pre-hell…is that any clearer?

VOID: (*Seriously.*) I'm sorry I really don't know. I'm not that well up on these things.

SUICIDE: You're not even educated. The Void is feeble-minded, obsequious, childish, boring and completely uneducated. Everything about him is all too familiar to me. The one thing he isn't is the one thing he ought to be…the Great Void. Look, sorry, this isn't easy for me, I was expecting something sublime, I can't help feeling that Eternity has rather let me down…

VOID: Everyone gets the Void they deserve.

SUICIDE: In that case there must have been a mix up somewhere along the line. I am the man who managed to create electrical images of people's dreams. I was the number one expert in the science of sleep, back there. I am the man who was developing the DVA, for God's sake, until shortly before its completion, but who wasn't allowed to complete it, not for want of wanting!

VOID: Yes, fine, but this Hugenstock, this lab assistant of yours, what was he like?

SUICIDE: It's plain that you're only really interested in people of your own kind. Hugenstock's just your sort of bloke. You would have got on like a house on fire. I worked to develop an apparatus by means of which one could actually display a man's dreams, the deepest recesses of his mind, actually project them visibly on a screen, actually record them, save them, and then play them back, like any old film on video. Does that go beyond your understanding? I tell you, it went way beyond mine…

VOID: No it's very interesting what you're saying. I'm listening I promise.

SUICIDE: Why am I bothering even speaking to you? You can have no concept of human existence. Man is a creature that eats, works and sleeps. Broadly speaking that is man's daily task. And when he sleeps, he dreams. We all do. Am I making myself clear?

VOID: Yeah, totally. I was just wondering what sort of guy Hugenstock was.

SUICIDE: You'll drive me mad. I'm trying to give you some sort of understanding of what a thinking, questing mind can achieve, of the terrifying boundaries the desire for the attainment of knowledge can bump you up against, and why, given certain circumstances, this desire led to that one momentous act which I was ultimately prepared to commit. I'm trying to give you some sort of understanding of how it was that I, at that fateful moment when I was standing in front of my almost completed Dream-video-adaptor, that I could have become in that existential instant the loneliest man on the entire planet.

VOID: But was Hugenstock there too?

SUICIDE: Hugenstock was not important! He was just this person, this student! Just one of the staff! Just an assistant, not even that good!

VOID: Still. Better than no one.

SUICIDE: Okay, look, fine. Whatever you say. I'm just trying not to get too close to you, that's all. I'm sorry. Sit down. I'm in a melancholy mood. I should tell you what happened. After much trial and error, I succeeded in

performing an experiment on myself, in which I was trying
to record an uninterrupted sequence of dreams lasting
the length of one complete night's sleep. And the next
morning I had a look at the utter carnage I'd recorded on
tape. My dear friend. Five hours after that, the whole thing
was over and done with. Everything. Gone, destroyed,
wiped out, annihilated. Everything, all the technological,
even spiritual advances that that devilish machine had
made possible, the software, the hardware, and then, to be
on the safe side, my own existence. In all the human race
not one trace left of my dream.

(*The VOID is jiggling his leg.*)

Obviously I'm boring you.

VOID: No not at all. I admire you very much. The whole
world does.

SUICIDE: Most of the time I was surrounded with yes-men,
arse-lickers. Who on closer acquaintance turned out to be
sadists. I've had enough of that. Enough of the 'normal
human weaknesses' that everyone seems so keen to
forgive. I don't forgive them.

VOID: You shouldn't be so harsh. If you're not prepared to
compromise, you'll never get on with anybody.

SUICIDE: I'm beginning to wonder what the point of ending
my life was if I have to put up with the same old platitudes
here as there.

VOID: You still seem to be railing against heaven. There's no
point in shaking your fist skywards any more. There's just
me here. Nothing in front, nothing behind. Nothing above,
nothing below. And here too, no one no one manages to
change anything. The only difference being that over here
you can try an infinite number of times…whereas over
there…

SUICIDE: There must be some activity we can engage in
without perpetually getting on each other's nerves.

VOID: Well to be honest, what? I mean, what else is there to
actually do here but talk to each other? Eating, sleeping,
dreaming. None of any of that here. So what does one
ultimately do? One talks. And I tell you, it could be worse.

SUICIDE: It couldn't! It's hell, total hell!

VOID: Well, yes, of course.

SUICIDE: And you're not going to leave me alone for a minute.

VOID: I couldn't, it's against my nature.

SUICIDE: In that case, we'll talk. We'll talk and talk till we reach the end of time.

VOID: We'll never actually do that.

SUICIDE: In that case till we reach insanity.

VOID: All we really do here is Stasis. That's all we've really got to offer. Insanity, and thingy…oh you know, what's the other -anity word? Something -anity. Erm…

SUICIDE: Vanity?

VOID: Nope.

SUICIDE: Urbanity, inanity, humanity, profanity, Christianity, manatee.

VOID: No, no, insanity and…grrr…tip of my tongue. No, it's gone. What I'm trying to say is that nothing seems to quite happen here. We don't seem to have the right climate for that. Got it. (*Finds the word.*) *Megalomania!* That's it. Insanity and megalomania. Like I said, they don't seem to quite happen here. Well, at least I remembered the word! I tell you, it can take half an eternity here, looking for a word you can't quite remember. Half an eternity it can take sometimes…

131

THE EVENING OF THE WEDDING

SHE sits miserably, in her wedding dress. HE has turned the collar of his dress suit up, and is dancing around her a bit, trying to cheer her up. Over the doors there are green hanging garlands.

SHE: Well, this is a fun evening.

HE: Doing the wedding tango!

SHE: Great. What kind of wedding is this anyway? Absolutely no one here. Not a soul. Not for miles around.

HE: I know. I know. But that's typical of us, isn't it? So bound up in our own happiness that we forget to invite anyone.

SHE: Any average birthday would be a sight jollier than this. And they happen every year.

HE: You've got another one coming up soon, haven't you?

SHE: No parents, no friends, not one single guest. Why didn't you invite anybody?

HE: I don't know anybody.

SHE: Since I've been with you I don't know anyone either.

HE: All that means is that for a while now we've been completely bound up in each other.

SHE: Yes you're right, that's what it means.

HE: Does that sadden you?

SHE: No it doesn't sadden me. Actually to be honest I don't really care that much one way or the other. It's just a bit of a puzzle, that's all.

HE: (*Touching the garlands.*) A puzzle. Okay. What's this? You hang them on a wall and they rustle a bit.

SHE: No, I mean it's a bit of a puzzle that not one single flower, not one single telegram, not one single letter of congratulation arrived. Did you really not tell a single soul that today was our wedding day?

HE: I didn't tell anyone because I don't know anyone.

SHE: Yes, but the fact absolutely nobody turned up is a different matter. That we really have to take personal responsibility for. The fact that we've completely cut ourselves off from everybody and everything.

HE: Plus the fact that our total and utter happiness must have been like a perpetual thorn in the flesh to our for former friends and acquaintances.

SHE: But it's a still a puzzle that no one sent anything. Are you sure you haven't hidden anything?

HE: Me? I promise you, nothing arrived. Which actually, basically, is pretty typical of us! As happy as Larry, and then when it comes to the actual day of the actual party we're standing around like idiots, without a single soul to show for it.

SHE: The day of the party. Actually that's the point. That's what's really bugging me. The fact that certain acquaintances aren't here, I can take. But there should at least be a party. And I think in this regard the two of us are not entirely above reproach.

HE: Well. The only thing I could still do is to invite a couple of complete strangers in off the street.

SHE: Complete strangers are rarely in the mood for a party. They'd just stand around and gawp at each other. You can tell that from what they're like in the street.

HE: Perhaps once they're in the house they might start to behave a little bit better than they do in the street. I think I could rustle up a party-type atmosphere fairly quickly.

SHE: Aren't you being slightly over-ambitious? It's been a few years now since you've actually met any complete strangers.

HE: Yes you're probably right. I'm out of practice, is that what you're saying? Fair enough, but you know, I have had dealings with complete strangers in my time. And I think the experience was basically satisfactory. I think I still know the right way to handle them. It should be okay.

SHE: The whole thing's still a mystery. The fact that no one's even rung. Go and check if the phone line's dead.

HE: (*Checking the phone.*) Nope. Phone line not dead. Phone line alive and kicking.

SHE: Or maybe we got the wrong day?

HE: Of our own wedding? We can't have done. *They* might have done, we didn't. We simply got married on the day we were always going to get married on.

SHE: Yes, but what day's that?

HE: The marriage was booked for today and today we got married.

SHE: Yes, you keep saying today. But what day is it today? I didn't see a calendar in the church, did you? The minister just marries whoever happens to turn up. Whoever points at him.

HE: We wanted to get married on the thirtieth of September, and that's what we did.

SHE: Is that today?

HE: Erm…um…

SHE: What day of the week is it?

HE: Well you'd assume it was a Saturday wouldn't you?

SHE: Is today a Saturday?

HE: Listen. Yesterday I was getting my hair cut. And someone there said, 'It's Friday today.' That's what I worked it out from. And I said, 'I'm getting married this weekend.' Big reaction. Great whooping amidst the clicking of scissors and the whooshing of hairdryers. Cries of 'Who's the lucky girl?', 'Where's the honeymoon?' All that…

SHE: This weekend… This weekend. That's the clue, that's the answer to all this. The weekend consists of two days, doesn't it? And today, my dear husband, is a Sunday. We got married on a Sunday.

HE: Why do you think that?

SHE: Because no one's phoned. The whole world thinks we got married on Saturday, like it says in your diary, and on Sunday we'd be off on our honeymoon.

HE: But no one rang yesterday either.

SHE: Yesterday, on your wedding day, you were at the hairdresser's. And I wasn't around at all, I hadn't yet moved in, as tradition demands. Yesterday is when they all rang, every one of them.

HE: Okay, say there's a man sitting next to you at the hairdresser's and he says loud and clear that today's Friday, and that was yesterday.

SHE: And you just believed him, some bloke who was just having his hair cut? People nowadays get their weekends completely confused. Friday, Saturday, Sunday? It's anyone's guess…just one great big time-off mish-mash.

HE: Well, okay. So we got married a day too late, big deal.

SHE: Too late?

HE: Yeah, later than we planned. It's not the end of the world though.

SHE: How could have that have happened?

HE: Because we were so happy all the time. Don't forget that.

SHE: Okay, yes, that firstly, but secondly because we let the Great Apathy into our lives.

HE: Yes you're right... We invited him in and told him to make himself at home, precisely because we were so happy.

SHE: That's why we were so in his thrall. That's why he organised us this totally defunct party. With no flowers. No telegrams of congratulation. No phone calls. And as for guests, forget it.

HE: Well if you're finding it so boring, why not just ring someone up and get them to congratulate us.

SHE: Me? Ring someone up? On my wedding day? If ever there were a day in my life when I would want to be the person being rung, as opposed to the person doing the ringing, then today is that day. Or yesterday. The day on which I was still unmarried and on which all telephonic congratulations, indeed phone calls of any sort, ricocheted off my rather old-fashioned insistence on being absent.

HE: Do you really think it was him, who kept all those people from us?

SHE: Who?

HE: The Great Apathy.

SHE: Yes. That's what I believe.

HE: If your parents were still around we wouldn't be sitting here waiting for a phone call, that's for sure.

SHE: You're surely not reproaching me for the fact that my parents aren't alive any more?

HE: It not reproaching you at all. I haven't got any parents any more either.

SHE: We knew we were both orphans before we decided to get married. You can't complain about it now.

HE: I wouldn't dream of it. It was in the full knowledge of our complete orphanhood that we decided to embark upon the road to matrimony... It was in the complete awareness of our parentless state that we decided to devote our lives to our continuing happiness.

SHE: Then stop complaining. We are now married, and I find it slightly insulting that we should be reminding each other of our orphanhood.

HE: Nevertheless, parents are still an important component of a day like this, a day on which their absence is all the more strongly felt.

SHE: Only because in all of God's wide world we don't seem to know anybody else. And because when we start wondering whom we should ask, or rather whom we should have asked to our wedding, we keep on coming back to our poor dead parents! And you, it has to be said, haven't exactly been busting a gut to guarantee your bride a suitable welcome in your house. There were no flowers from you either. No music did you provide. No majestically laden table. No nothing.

HE: You keep on forgetting the fact that we were quite simply too happy – well at least I was, I can only speak for myself – for too happy to even think about such practicalities. Even so, I did make an effort and hung up these garlands. For all the thanks I've got.

SHE: You hung up the garlands?

HE: I did hang up these garlands, yes.

SHE: You really think that this is the first time I've seen these garlands?

HE: Well, okay, you may or may not have seen these or similar garlands at some time in the past. Granted.

SHE: You hung them up that time when we had our first brandy together.

HE: Really? I don't remember.

SHE: In fact, you hang these particular garlands up on a fairly regular basis whenever the mood happens to take you. On every special, or in fact not so very special occasion.

HE: Those 'not so very special occasions' as you call them, which I've been tempted to enliven by hanging up these particular garlands, I can count on the fingers of one hand. My birth, my parents' death, our wedding day. And okay, maybe also the first time you had a brandy in my house.

SHE: My point is that these garlands do not necessarily betoken anything that remarkable.

HE: Well it might be remarkable, say, if I were to tear them down.

SHE: No, don't do that.

HE: I'm sick of the sight of them...

SHE: I can understand that.

HE: A garland on which aspersions have been cast is, as I see it, no better than a wreath. Tear it down I say!

SHE: No. Don't. They're the only party decorations we've got. And you might consider that the only thing remarkable about them is that they're hanging there just as they were on the evening we first drank brandy together, an evening not unconnected with today's events.

HE: I have no choice but to tell you that because of the fact that, from now on, I can relate to these garlands (your totally bogus personifications of which I have now comprehensively seen through) neither through the backdoor of mawkish sentimentality, nor on the crutches of some lame sort of sympathetic sort of compromise...that these garlands will never, for me, be the thing that they were.

SHE: And nor will we, my love, nor will we...

HE: What's that supposed to mean? I was under the impression we were on the threshold of an all-embracing life partnership. I refuse to let some tatty old garland acquire completely spurious symbolic significance. If these garlands serve only to remind you of those same garlands which happened to be hanging there, or so you claim, at some putative moment in the past, then they will have *completely* failed in fulfilling the function for which they are hanging here to day, to wit as a signpost which marks the beginning of a shared future hitherto un-embarked on. And I mean completely.

SHE: Those poor pathetic garlands. How sadly they hang there now. To look at them, and to listen to you...well, so much for 'bless this house', so much for domestic bliss.

HE: I'm going to have to ask you to spare me this provocative, hypocritical nonsense. Oh yes, she finds it all too easy to be self-pitying and melodramatic, as a pathetic and all too obvious attempt to score sympathy points for herself. And I'm sure she easily can drum up a quorum of gullible adherents whom she can impress with her romantic symbolism.

SHE: You're particularly harsh with me this evening. You've never taken this tone with me before.

HE: Well, even if I… Anyway, you're a bitch!

SHE: If you get this upset about a harmless set of garlands, what are you going to be like when I finally introduce Selma, my tortoise, into the household?

HE: That's not fair, I love Selma!

SHE: You say that now, but you don't yet know what it's like in the mornings, when you're still half asleep and trying to shave and she starts crawling over your bare feet. I'd like to hear what you say about her then.

HE: You have to admit there's a world of difference between a garland which on one's wedding day, with all its implicit pros and cons, threatens to crush a happy couple like a boa constrictor, and a cute little tortoise nuzzling affectionately up to some guy's toes as he's standing by his washbasin.

SHE: Yes. Of course, you're right. I'm just wondering whether or not they'll get on. Selma and the garlands.

HE: And the…? Are you *really* wondering that…I mean seriously?

SHE: I am, yes, seriously wondering that.

(*The sound of an alarm. OFFICE WORKERS cross from one door to another.*)

IDOLS

GIRL: It's you, isn't it?

MAN: Me? No? What do you mean?

GIRL: I know you!

MAN: Well maybe off the telly. I was on *Name That Tune* one
time.

*(The GIRL walks round the inner circle of the doors. On the
outside a man's shadow is seen to be following her.)*

GIRL: I can't go anywhere round here without thinking of
Burning Tears. You know what I mean? It's like we're
all walking round stuck in Raining March. Knackered,
wired, like in the Dick Mobby show. You know what I
mean? And as far as the future's concerned, all I have to
say is Peggy Horn. Enough said. You know what I mean?
It's all phoney, isn't it, everything's false, fake. It's like
everything's Falstaff meets Doctor Sauerbach, that's what I
think anyway. Okay I know that sounds a bit like Stokely
Nightmare, granted, but it's still true. Most of us go round
thinking we're some sort of Samuel Hotchkins, but the
truth is we're more like some kind of pathetic kind of Nick
McBone. If they had a bit more Liza Battlestrong in their
veins you wouldn't spot them straight away as some sort of
sub-genus of Flower Broker. Ah well. Not everyone can be
as clear and articulate as Lou in the Sun....

*(A door opens. A YOUNG MAN in overalls appears, backlit, and
stands provocatively in the doorway.)*

(Quietly, to the YOUNG MAN.) Get me out of here. Help me!
In reality I'm really clever. I compose letters. I read tarot
cards.

*(She exits through the door the YOUNG MAN is holding open.
Blackout. Music: Talking Heads.*

*Lights up again. The GIRL is now carrying a TWA bag and
sitting on a park bench with the MAN in the middle of the
stage.)*

MAN: How did you meet that guy?

GIRL: Mark used to be the personal photographer of the
drummer off of Talking Heads. So, very close to the
proverbial throne. At first it was like this big love affair,

but then he started trying to turn me into something else. I was way too young and just let everything sort of happen. Also he'd invested all my money. I've got shares now in Siemens, and in Daimler. Actually I should find out how they're getting on. No! Never again. Too much like hard work. It only ever happened 'cos my mate Andreas disappeared. And that's not the first time it's happened to me either. One day they just piss off, God knows where, with God knows who and you never see them again. For instance, this friend of mine, this girl, she had a kid with this Egyptian guy. Five years he stayed with her, and really cared for her. And then one day he just pissed off. She didn't hear a peep out of him. She searched everywhere. Cairo. Then the town he was born in. Put ads in the papers, got in touch with the police, you name it. I tell you, Egyptians, once they've gone you're never going to find them again.

MAN: What are we going to do now?

GIRL: Dunno. Tell me something. Do you really know about investments?

MAN: Not that much. I just wanted to get you out of a mess.

GIRL: No, that's great. Now I know where I am.

MAN: How old are you?

GIRL: Nineteen.

MAN: What about your parents?

GIRL: They're not interested in what I'm doing. You saved my life.

MAN: Don't exaggerate!

GIRL: No really, honestly. They would have completely killed me in there.

MAN: I have to go home. My wife's expecting me.

GIRL: Why don't we go to a hotel. I'd like to find some way of showing my gratitude.

(Lights change. All the doors open. In the background the sounds of a lively party. Lights fully up. The park bench that the MAN and the GIRL were sitting on has now been extended and is covered with people. At least eight, some costumed. From the left to the right, the WOMAN, two Dominican monks BROTHER

JOHANN and BROTHER FREDDY, the GIRL, COLOMBINE, the LADY WITH THE MICROPHONE, the CONTENTED WOMAN, EMPEROR JULIAN, the MAN, the QUIET GUY.)

ON THE LONG BENCH

GIRL: (*Talking to the MAN, who is sitting four people away from her.*)
So, two nights, and one day. The first night, the first day,
the second night…and now, what? Your conscience, is that
it? 'I wish it'd never happened'? Is that it?

MAN: I don't know.

GIRL: You don't know. I see.
(*She takes a bottle of wine from her TWA bag, pours some into
a cardboard cup, and drinks.*)

MAN: And anyhow, what do you mean by 'happened'?

GIRL: Exactly.

BROTHER JOHANN: (*Showing BROTHER FREDDY a photo.*)
Here's where we jump out of hell. Huge columns of
sulphur. Dragon's venom.
(*BROTHER FREDDY looks at the picture, uninterestedly, and
passes it on. It gets variously passed on as the scene continues.*)

MAN: (*Sighing.*) Oh Christ…

GIRL: Weird feeling, isn't it?

MAN: Yeah. Weird.

GIRL: My God!

MAN: How about you?

GIRL: Me? I'm sad. Just really really deep down sad.

MAN: Hmm. I understand.

GIRL: Oh, you understand do you? Oh good. (*She drinks.*)
Nevertheless. Thank you. It was fantastic.

MAN: My God. Why is everything so complicated?

GIRL: No really, I mean it. Thank you. I've never known
anything like it. I feel…I felt so close to you. And I don't
find that complicated at all. I feel amazingly close to you.
That's rather simple, isn't it?

MAN: Yes, okay.

GIRL: Except…?

MAN: You're not someone who makes people happier.

GIRL: So, what, it was all nothing? You…

MAN: Shhh! Not so loud.

GIRL: So we had thirty-six wasted hours? Is that what you're
saying?

BROTHER JOHANN: Look, here. Here's where it suddenly plummets right down. That's where the illiterate and lazy are flailing in the mud. That's where the horses stand around with their blank eyes, pale as the moon...
(*He passes the photo on...*)

EMPEROR JULIAN: I can still get angry at pictures like this. They can still provoke me to massive rage. I'm one of the few remaining people who, after looking at such pictures, would be prepared to declare war.

LADY WITH THE MICROPHONE: (*Holding the microphone to the CONTENTED WOMAN.*) And who are you?

CONTENTED WOMAN: My name is Henrietta Rombach. I'm twenty-nine years old. I work as a laboratory assistant. I'm single. I live with my parents, but in my own room in a two and a half bedroom apartment. My hobbies are travel, animals, history, and as you can probably see, I love going to the theatre.

COLOMBINE: (*Into the microphone.*) My name is Colombine. I'm four hundred and thirteen years old. Also single. I love straw hats, intrigues, and the clatter of tea cups.

GIRL: And I'm not going to give up. I'm going to keep on asking you. What are you doing? What are you doing to me?

MAN: I want to go my own way. What's wrong with that?

GIRL: Everything!

LADY WITH THE MICROPHONE: Okay. The topic is history. Emperor Julian...

EMPEROR JULIAN: History? No. Nothing's historical. Everything's actual.

LADY WITH THE MICROPHONE: Yes, but surely the human race has somewhat developed since the days when you were on the throne...

EMPEROR JULIAN: Human beings shouldn't really discuss the human race. They have no true understanding thereof. Next question?

LADY WITH THE MICROPHONE: (*Leafing through her notebook.*) Erm...I don't know...that's all the questions I seem to have...

EMPEROR JULIAN: Come on. Questions. More questions. Otherwise I cannot speak. You want to lead me into the desert and let me die of thirst?

LADY WITH THE MICROPHONE: Oh for heaven's sake, *someone* must have a question for the Emperor Julian?

BROTHER JOHANN: We could all think of questions to ask him. Nothing easier. We just don't want to, that's all. Emperor of the Heathens! We hope he roasts in the pit of hell, unquestioned for all eternity!

EMPEROR JULIAN: The divine is scattered on us all equally. So stop complaining, photographer!

COLOMBINE: Why do you ask questions, when you're not that interested in the answers?

LADY WITH THE MICROPHONE: Oh please! I ask question after question so as never to have to answer.

GIRL AND OTHERS: Who are you? Who are you?

LADY WITH THE MICROPHONE: No! No! Don't ask me questions. Don't do it!

QUIET GUY: I'm the sort of guy who is never satisfied. A bolt of energy. A powerful compact package of sheer will and pure imagination. A nasty bitchy dinner party, embodied in one man.

GIRL: You could at least write down my phone number.

MAN: I've got nothing to write with.

(*GIRL gets a biro out of her handbag and passes it along to him.*)

GIRL: Write it on your wrist: 773-1358.

QUIET GUY: I hope it stays on.

COLOMBINE: (*To BROTHER FREDDY.*) Among your saints, have you got one of those artist saints? You know the sort I mean. You show them an ornament or an art work, and if they start to weep, it's genuine. If they don't, it's just fake tat.

LADY WITH THE MICROPHONE: (*To the CONTENTED WOMAN.*) Did you say just now that you lived on your own?

CONTENTED WOMAN: Oh yes!

LADY WITH THE MICROPHONE: You'll forgive me for prying, but is that the way you wanted it, or is it just the way it worked out?

CONTENTED WOMAN: It suits me better, being on my own. I find I get more from life when I'm independent.

LADY WITH THE MICROPHONE: Even with the silence in the evenings, and not a soul to talk to?

CONTENTED WOMAN: Oh, I can always speak to things. Plus things seem to like me. I'm not clumsy, I don't break stuff. I've never yet once dropped a vase or a plate. Honestly, I've never ever broken anything. I'm happy...no, to be precise, I'm very contented. That's what I am. If I were happy, I'd almost certainly have dropped something.

MAN: Is it hard for you now?

GIRL: How can you ask me that!?

MAN: Well...you know...

BROTHER FREDDY: That can't have been all of them...?

BROTHER JOHANN: (*Looking through the pictures, uneasily.*) Not all of them? What more do you want? Look, here, here's the possessed horse. Here's the ripped up bird. The bile-green philosopher. The melting eyes. What more do you want? Here are the collapsing towers. And here's the year dot.

Blackout.

TIME AND THE ROOM

Characters

FRANK ARNOLD
also FIRST MAN in Act Two

COMPLETE STRANGER
also SECOND MAN/GRAPHIC ARTIST in Act Two

MARIE STEUBER
also EXECUTIVE in Act Two

MAN IN A WINTER COAT
also RUDOLPH in the 'Medea' scene, CUSTOMER in
Act Two and THIRD MAN

JULIUS
who lives with

OLAF

MAN WITH NO WATCH (ANSGAR)

IMPATIENT WOMAN
also COLLEAGUE in Act Two

SLEEPWOMAN
also the BOSS of the office in Act Two

The voice of the PILLAR

MAN AT WINDOW

This translation of *Time and the Room* was first performed on 27 August 1996 at the Royal Lyceum Theatre, Edinburgh in a production directed by Martin Duncan and designed by Wolfgang Göbbel.

Act One

A room. Three big windows looking out onto the street. In the background a façade of the house opposite. In front of the middle window a small table and two chairs. One facing the window, one facing the room. On the left a door to the rest of the apartment and a pillar clad in wood. JULIUS on the chair looking out, OLAF on the other one.

JULIUS: You haven't looked out of the window yet today. The Christmas trees are still lying there by the side of the road…and it's February. Heaps of sand fringed with tongues of ice, like artificial leaves. The burnt out fireworks from New Year's Eve are beginning to reappear through the melting snow. And last year's dog shit. Sparrows are pecking away at the bobbles on the plane trees, blindly, nervously. The squeal of tyres, drivers take their car batteries indoors for the night to keep them warm. Pigeons' claws scrabbling away at the metal window ledges. Worthless birds. Garbage – the garbage of the skies. No peace, no quiet anywhere. A general sleepy murmur and above it the rasping snore of pneumatic drills. Hard to say what sort of day it is. Could easily be the brownest, muggiest day of the year. Girls give a quick glance at their reflections in shop windows, giving their hair a cursory brush as they scurry past. Here comes one now. Knee length skirt (she must be freezing), black tights. She's puffing into the collar of her pullover, green with gold lamé. Not pretty, not at all. You can tell her at a glance by the way she walks, sluttish, slovenly, been leafing through too many crappy magazines, curling her hair, her face is pale as her TV screen.

Those young men next door are wandering around in their dirty overalls and dungarees. They're still doing up the house round the back. The state-assisted unemployed – thick heavy key rings on their belts – lots of keys. They're loading and unloading little hire vans, driving forklift truck loads of insulating stuff through the gates. They work seven days a week and every night they're down the pub with their wives and their Alsatians and they seem happy enough. Half of them used to own places themselves – half of them are about to.

(The door buzzer goes. JULIUS presses a button under the window ledge. The girl from the street, MARIE STEUBER, enters.)

MARIE STEUBER: Were you talking about me just now? Was it you? What were you saying? Leafing through crappy magazines, curling my hair, my face as pale as my TV, you don't know me at all. You look out the window, you see me for the first time and come up with these pejorative snap judgements. What do you know about me? Nothing.

(She goes to the left hand window and looks out into the street.)

When I arrived at the airport, the carousel thing was chock-a-block with suitcases, all identical. No one could find their stuff. In the end I picked up any old case. I couldn't be bothered jostling about with two hundred and fifty hysterical passengers. In Arrivals I saw this bloke who looked like he was waiting to meet me, to pick me up, so I said to him, 'Are you Frank Arnold?' He said yes. But he wasn't. He was just this bloke who hangs around the airport every day on the lookout for people who look like they're waiting to be picked up. And whatever name they say, he says yes.

(She lights a cigarette and leaves her disposable cigarette-lighter on the window-sill.)

Of course I've adapted myself to everybody. I've had to. To the boring old fart, to the shy sensitive type, to the businessman. I've shared their problems, their nature, their views on life. I've pondered it, accepted it, and ultimately made it my own. I've answered their questions, all of them. The chatty ones, the strong silent types. To the unhappy I've been a helping hand, to the exuberant I've been the giggling friend. I've gone jogging with the sporty type, gone boozing with the boozy type. No effort spared, no stone left unturned. Not with any of them. Which was healthy. And good. I could give it, I could take it, I could leave it. The thing that I am. *(Surveys room.)* Haven't you got a thermometer barometer rain gauge?

JULIUS: We have got quite a feel for the weather here. When he's looking out of the window and I'm facing the room, then it's going to rain or snow. When I'm looking out of the window and he's facing the room it means the sun will soon start shining.

(*Door buzzer sounds. Enter the MAN WITH NO WATCH. He searches around.*)

MAN WITH NO WATCH: I was at a party here last night. I must have left my wristwatch somewhere here. It was here, wasn't it? Yes, I remember this room precisely, those three big windows looking out onto the street. Do you mind if I have a look in the bathroom?

JULIUS: Feel free.

(*MAN WITH NO WATCH exits through the door on the right.*)

MARIE STEUBER: Well, to return to the…as I was saying, in this life we've really only got our memories. Everything else is just standing by the window – looking out. Until we vanish from the face of the earth.

(*Doorbell. Enter the IMPATIENT WOMAN. The MAN WITH NO WATCH pops his head through the right-hand door.*)

IMPATIENT WOMAN: I wanted to see you again.

MAN WITH NO WATCH: (*Entering.*) What a strange coincidence! I came here to look for something I lost. How are you?

IMPATIENT WOMAN: Fine. I didn't sleep very well.

MAN WITH NO WATCH: Nor did I. There was something kind of…and this morning when I woke up I felt, I felt as if I'd lost something.

IMPATIENT WOMAN: I felt as if I'd won something.

MAN WITH NO WATCH: I woke up and wanted to look at my watch. Which is when I noticed it wasn't on my bedside table. So I've been looking for it.

IMPATIENT WOMAN: And? And? Did you find it?

MAN WITH NO WATCH: No. I'm not really sure that this is where I lost it.

IMPATIENT WOMAN: Odd. Your behaviour to me is quite different to yesterday evening.

MAN WITH NO WATCH: Yes, true. Yesterday I was still quite reticent.

IMPATIENT WOMAN: No, it wasn't that. You weren't reticent at all. Far from it. You were very attentive. Quite overwhelming me with compliments.

MAN WITH NO WATCH: Well, in the meantime I've got a little closer to you and now perhaps now I'm taking liberties. Or so it seems to me.

IMPATIENT WOMAN: And I get the impression that you feel uncomfortable with me. As if I bored you. You're not behaving like you did yesterday evening.

MAN WITH NO WATCH: You must think me very importunate.

IMPATIENT WOMAN: No, not at all. I wasn't hoping for anything else.

MAN WITH NO WATCH: Strange. And I was thinking, 'Now you've gone and pushed it too far. Now you're being a nuisance.'

IMPATIENT WOMAN: No, you're not the man you were yesterday.

MAN WITH NO WATCH: Really? Oh, by the way, do you know what the time is?

(*They go to the window and look out.*)

JULIUS: You see, Olaf, how these little people can get everything wrong. Get everything muddled up. There never was a party here. Not last night. Not the night before. Nor a year ago, and probably not since the first housewarming ever – never.

(*Doorbell.*

FRANK ARNOLD enters, with an airport sign.)

FRANK ARNOLD: Sorry to disturb you, but is there a Marie Steuber here?

(*MARIE STEUBER turns round on the window ledge.*)

Are you her? I was only five minutes late at the airport but by then you'd gone off with someone else. Pity. Gentlemen, this woman is a joker in the pack. Any one can play her at any time for their own purposes. So farewell, Marie Steuber. You would have been spared everything that's going to happen to you from now on if you'd only waited five more minutes for me. We've missed each other, Marie. You could have been in my pack of cards.

(*Exits through the left-hand door.*

MAN WITH NO WATCH goes to MARIE STEUBER.)

MAN WITH NO WATCH: I heard about it. It must have been awful for you.

MARIE STEUBER: You heard about it? I'll tell you about it myself, if you'd rather.

MAN WITH NO WATCH: It must have been ghastly.

MARIE STEUBER: They can almost restore you to health, you know. Cure you, sort of. Of course your looks suffer, as you can see. That's not fat, that's not alcohol, that's the pills, that's the drugs. That crap from the chemist.

MAN WITH NO WATCH: But do you want to live now?

MARIE STEUBER: First of all they gave me a blocker which affected my motor activity. So I had these involuntary spasms, throwing my arms up, you know, like 'don't shoot, don't shoot' – so obviously I did want to live, yes, very much.

MAN WITH NO WATCH: The way you talk about it now's like you were telling some sort of funny story at the office.

MARIE STEUBER: Then they tried out a new medicine on me which made me repeat everything anyone said. So I never answered anyone's questions, I just repeated the sounds I thought I heard. I became an echo.

MAN WITH NO WATCH: But were you completely conscious?

MARIE STEUBER: The alternative was the treatment which would have made me clutch at everything like a baby. Grab, grab, grab.

(She grabs the IMPATIENT WOMAN whom curiosity has drawn close by, by the arm. She draws back with a cry – 'Ouch.')

MAN WITH NO WATCH: You can live through sickness. Over the years. Just like a tree which manages to isolate a wound from its organism, it shuts it off but retains it as dead wood, a dead appendage. But the tree grows on, around it and past it. And you will also grow.

MARIE STEUBER: I've tried it twice. Given it my best shot. I cannot live. And I'll try it a third time, if I have to and if I've got the strength. The thing inside me, the elephant that wants to trample me to death, has been knocked out with stun bullets, but only temporarily. One day it'll wake up in the zoo.

155

(*MAN WITH NO WATCH goes up to IMPATIENT WOMAN.*)

IMPATIENT WOMAN: You were talking to Marie? God, I'd feel
really nervous talking to her. How do you talk to someone
who's been through something like that?

MAN WITH NO WATCH: I feel that I had something to say to
her. Which she's probably reflecting on now. I gave her a
metaphor for her illness which I think will make it easier
to live with. You have to pick the right words. Sensitive
words. Providing, I hope, positive vibrations for someone
as sick as she is.

IMPATIENT WOMAN: I could never do that.

(*Lights, hurriedly, a cigarette.*)

MAN WITH NO WATCH: Yes, it's always better to confront these
issues head on.

JULIUS: (*Looking out of window, to OLAF.*) We don't want
anything. We have no plans. We're just two old sceptics
who are fond of each other. How long is it since we said,
'We could, we should, we must'? We share each other's
peace of mind, we enjoy each other's inner beauty. But
sometimes we've a plan – just on the tip of the tongue. So
near, so far. Or an idea, twinkling in the eye. But ideas are
shy things. The first hint of a sound or a word – they've
vanished. A plan can never be grasped – not by us. It's
ungraspable. If you think it through, meticulously. If you
consider every possible ramification. And basically we
don't want anything. Which, if you think about it, itself has
all sorts of far-reaching implications.

(*IMPATIENT WOMAN near MAN WITH NO WATCH by right
window.*)

IMPATIENT WOMAN: Often when I'm smoking I think, what I
need is a cigarette.

MAN WITH NO WATCH: How many do you smoke a day?

IMPATIENT WOMAN: Why do you ask?

MAN WITH NO WATCH: In order not to have to give answers.

IMPATIENT WOMAN: Yes, ask me. Ask me everything. Ask
me, ask me! Here, here, interrogate me. Only when you
ask, only then can I breathe, can I live.

MARIE STEUBER: (*Half looking out of the window.*) A man
carried a woman through the winter night, out of a hotel

which was on fire. She was sleeping in his arms, she slept through all the noise and the panic and the roar of the fire. She slept, she slept. He went home and took her with him. On the train she slept next to him, leaning against his shoulder. He took her to his house. She slept on a settee in his living room and she didn't wake up. He called doctors, they came and examined her but they couldn't, they wouldn't wake her up. They merely established the fact that she was healthy, healthy and asleep. So he carried on living with her by his side and gradually he understood. He was her dream, and nothing more. He became older and less sure of anything.

MAN WITH NO WATCH: What's that you're playing with on your wrist?

IMPATIENT WOMAN: Swatch. New brand of watch. You can have lots of them, for different uses, you can swap them around. Or collect them, or throw them away.

MAN WITH NO WATCH: Bet they'll invent watches for one day's use only. Like disposable razors, plastic knives and forks.

IMPATIENT WOMAN: In this brand you can get all sorts. Watches for ski jumping, saunas, table-turning, love at first sight, afternoons at the dolphinarium. Even watches for specific hours of the day.
(*Doorbell.*

MAN IN A WINTER COAT enters, carrying in his arms a scantily-clad sleeping woman.)

MAN IN A WINTER COAT: God what a dreadful night. I didn't sleep a wink.

JULIUS: It's okay – we know all about it. Lay the woman down on the settee. We'll look after her.

MAN IN A WINTER COAT: Sir, your address was in the purse around her neck. You're obviously part of her circle of close friends.
(*JULIUS takes one of the SLEEPWOMAN's fingers, examines it closely.*)

JULIUS: Is it her or is it not? The finger rather scrawny. The top joint bent slightly upwards. Deep grooves by the bulge, there. Yes. Could be. Fingers which have always somehow

remained 'fingery'. Never quite been a real hand. Sprung
dactyls. But yes. I do remember. A long time ago – short
but sweet.

MAN IN A WINTER COAT: Amazing. All seven floors of this
ghastly hotel were on fire, completely burnt out. But no
one got hurt. All three hundred and twenty-eight guests
were woken up by the blaze, at four in the morning and
were either able to make their own way to safety or had to
wait to be rescued from the windows by the Fire Brigade.
But I grabbed hold of this woman who was sleeping on
a couch in the hall on the second floor, which was as it
happens also my floor, and spending the night for some
unfathomable reason known only to herself right opposite
the door to my room; and plainly sleeping far more deeply
than any of the other guests who were screaming past her
and streaming down the stairs.

(*He goes to the door, then turns.*)

If it's true that a man carries a woman inside him, who
is asleep, at the base of his spine and is called 'she who
lies wounded' or 'our Diana' then this is how it was that
she jumped into my arms, from inside me, on this night
of fire and I carried her, sleeping, hardly clothed, as she
was, from this house of flames. And from now on I will
never forget the sweet weight of her in repose, her naked
thigh pressing against the bones of my lower arm – the
fleshliness of this pure, chaste burden will weigh on my
soul for ever.

(*Exit.*)

JULIUS: That was a lovely trip. Up north. Thatched cottage
right by the sand dunes. In bed all day then out in the
evenings, unsteady on our pins, to buy our wine and soda
water. All in all a short time. Young girl. Always giggling,
always in a rush, embarrassed. Haven't heard of her since.
Never have dreamed that she'd've kept my address in
the purse round her neck. Travelled, suffered, gone on
pilgrimages. Died of love, found peace and died of love
again. No more beginnings. No more 'well I must be
going, the party's over'. You can say of happiness no more
hurry, never again. Our memory becomes so hard hearted

– looking at the finger of a long lost beloved. As if half
nakedness could seduce us into pronouncing half truths.
(*OLAF gets out of his chair – to stretch his legs. IMPATIENT
WOMAN gets off the window ledge and goes to him.*)

IMPATIENT WOMAN: We knew each other once.
(*OLAF turns back and sits down again. IMPATIENT WOMAN
goes back to the window.*)
No. That was terrible. I'll try it again.
(*OLAF gets up again. IMPATIENT WOMAN tries again.*)
We knew each other once…
(*OLAF turns back, sits down again. IMPATIENT WOMAN goes
to window.*)
No. I haven't got it yet. I'll try again later…

MARIE STEUBER: (*Half looking out of the window.*) Between
people there's this sickening crunch and the whole
machine grinds to a halt. Then they all go somersaulting
forwards, falling head over heels over each other, onwards
in their own straight lines. Then silence, like iron.

JULIUS: Careful. Don't talk about it or it will happen.

MARIE STEUBER: Some of them push their table in front of the
window or the cupboard by the bed. They move the odd
thing around in their flats or they carry clean washing from
one room to another. Or they duck as they hurry past their
mirrors. And then it goes very quiet.

JULIUS: Careful. Don't talk about it, or it'll happen.

MARIE STEUBER: Opposite on the third floor a woman wakes
up late in an unfamiliar flat, takes her first look out of the
window, reads a newspaper that's lying around, makes
some coffee, can't find the sugar, wipes the stains off the
kitchen table, sneezes into the dishcloth, takes a phone call
that's nothing to do with her, has a bath, opens her second
travelling bag and then she too leaves everything as it was.
(*Doorbell. The COMPLETE STRANGER enters quickly, goes to
the SLEEPWOMAN.*)

COMPLETE STRANGER: Has she told you anything? I'm
asking you? Has she mentioned anything? Dropped any
hints?

ALL: No.

COMPLETE STRANGER: You don't know who I am?

159

ALL: No.

COMPLETE STRANGER: You speak with one voice. That ought to convince me. I wouldn't really know what I would have done with her. I wouldn't really know what I would have been capable of – Ectoplasm?

ALL: What?

COMPLETE STRANGER: Ectoplasm? Doesn't mean anything to you?

ALL: No.

COMPLETE STRANGER: Good. Then you really don't know who I am.

IMPATIENT WOMAN: You look like someone who when he was a little boy always had his pockets stuffed with odds and ends. Bits of string, penknives, tiddlywinks, india rubbers, mousetraps, pistol caps, magnifying glass, marbles, compass…

COMPLETE STRANGER: (*Slaps her.*) Shut up! It's too serious for you to make jokes about it. I can really do without your twinkly eyes thank you very much. What are you up to? Bloody nerve! One more word out of you and you'll have me to reckon with.

IMPATIENT WOMAN: No. Please. Here – take it. Take it all.
(*She removes her rings and bracelets, other jewellery falls out of her sleeves.*)
Take it – I'm fed up with it.
(*COMPLETE STRANGER takes it and puts it all in his pocket. Then he takes the SLEEPWOMAN and carries her out of the room.*)

JULIUS: So. There we are. She's gone again. Suddenly. Just like before. It's the rhythm of a door, that's all. Open shut. Open shut. Life is slammed to. And that's also the way it was then.
(*IMPATIENT WOMAN sits in the empty chair – turns to OLAF.*)

IMPATIENT WOMAN: Have you got some sort of cloth?

OLAF: No.

IMPATIENT WOMAN: Just a little cloth'll do.

OLAF: No.

IMPATIENT WOMAN: Just, you know, to wipe my forehead.

OLAF: No.

IMPATIENT WOMAN: It's very warm...or something.

OLAF: No.

JULIUS: The only sort of guest I'm really scared of is the one commonly known as the returning quest. A good hour after the end of a party, it's late. People have gone home, there he is, standing at the door, everything's been cleared away and he's back, back at the table, hand trembling, trying to start something or other all over again, as if he'd never been away. Come to give his opinion on some pointless, useless, trivial topic. You're dropping with fatigue but you have to bring back the old fruit, the cheese board, the half-empty bottle of red wine...

IMPATIENT WOMAN: They've all left their disposable lighters on the window sill. They won't be coming back.

(*The MAN WITH NO WATCH stands next to MARIE STEUBER by the window.*)

MARIE STEUBER: (*Looking out of the window.*) An old man's popping leaflets on the windscreens of the parked cars. Now he slips and falls into the gutter. Blood on his face – the ambulance will come along shortly to take him away. The man with the plastic hip-joint drags himself into the porno shop. The man in the wheelchair lets himself be carried in. Not a flicker of lust on their faces. Reluctantly, morosely, they wander in, and they come out with pale indifferent, cheesy faces, more like they've been to the bank, carrying away their videocassettes in brown plastic bags. On the street they don't even glance at women's bottoms – they don't look up, nor will they until they're safely home.

(*Ambulance siren getting nearer.*)

Look at them, all hurrying along. All out of step with each other. All running about, aimlessly, the hithering and thithering of the city, the mad scrimmage, places to go, things to do. It's all restless unease, fear of the big violent *crunch* – when they'll all stand still once and for all. Behind the most imperious military stride – I see a dilatory shuffle. In the brisk business-like step I see the image of an ambling layabout. In every brawling brat, the silence of the listening dead.

MAN WITH NO WATCH: Tell me. What did we want from each other? We must at some time or other have wanted something, something specific from each other? What was it?

MARIE STEUBER: I remember it very well. You had this real need to sleep with me. I mean there and then. We didn't know where to go. We ran into an apartment building. In the hall we met this old man who immediately took us under his wing. 'Cause at the back of the courtyard there was apparently this baroque palace, hidden away, with all sorts of historical treasures in it. And desire just melted away as we became lost in wonder at the works of history.

MAN WITH NO WATCH: I think you're wrong. We never slept with each other.

MARIE STEUBER: That's true. We never got round to it. Because after that we were busy wandering through history.

(*Shortly after, they exit together stage right.*)

JULIUS: I should have gone out more at night. I've never really 'let myself go'. I really should have 'gone for it more'. I didn't. I should have had a thousand more disappointments. As Swift says, I was born to know a million disappointments. And how many have I known? Not even a round dozen. I've grown more and more cautious. That's about all. But what's the point? Of living at the very limits of caution? One day you won't be able to hear rain fall without holding your head in your hands in total utter helpless despair.

(*Enter stage right SLEEPWOMAN in a summer dress. Stands by JULIUS at the window.*)

SLEEPWOMAN: Did you think that I was no more?

JULIUS: Where have you come from?

SLEEPWOMAN: I've been about you for a long time now. But you didn't notice.

JULIUS: Dinah, how did you find the long way back to my side?

SLEEPWOMAN: Dreaming of magnificent ballrooms, filled with the wind of hot summer nights which…

JULIUS: Oh yeah, sure. Look they found my address in your purse. Why did you want to come back to me?

SLEEPWOMAN: I don't remember. I don't know any more…

JULIUS: You must have wanted something from us.

SLEEPWOMAN: From you, yes.

JULIUS: There's two of us now.

SLEEPWOMAN: I don't know. Perhaps I lived the whole of last year in that hotel, the one which burnt down last night, and perhaps I had your address to hand in case of emergencies.

JULIUS: Did you start the fire Dinah?

SLEEPWOMAN: I haven't yet given it a thought, Julius.

JULIUS: We, Olaf and I, are racking our brains trying to make sense of the whole story.

SLEEPWOMAN: I feel I can only be of the very, very slightest assistance.

JULIUS: You're not asleep any more.

SLEEPWOMAN: No. Now I'm not asleep any more.

JULIUS: Not at all? How long will you be able to keep that up?

SLEEPWOMAN: How can I tell? How do I know whether it'll suit me?

JULIUS: You are here again, I've seen you again and you've shattered all my memories of you. You were a pillar of my past life – the terrible things you have to go through in your youth and now you come back and the pillar's been pulled away.

SLEEPWOMAN: The rift didn't hold. Over the years its edges grew back together again. The rift has healed.

IMPATIENT WOMAN: This cat, right, which I got to know once on my summer holidays, on Fehmarm, the other day I found it lying outside my front door, miaowing. Which, let's face it, is extremely improbable, isn't it, that five years later a cat – a cat you met on an island – is going to track you down and turn up and turn up and say hello. Almost impossible. Happened though. Till today I couldn't work out what it was about her (the cat) that made such a deep impression. But there must have been something special, to drive her to such an amazing feat, one that made complete nonsense of the laws of nature.

SLEEPWOMAN: (*Continuing to speak to JULIUS.*) I'm still convinced that that day you just said the wrong thing by accident. So you said 'farewell' by mistake. You could just as easily have said 'stay' or 'I'm yours'. No, you were looking for a phrase that would be conclusive, life-changing. You just picked the wrong one, that's all.

IMPATIENT WOMAN: (*Hits the SLEEPWOMAN clumsily on the shoulder.*) You lucky bitch! Little rich girl! Born with a silver spoon. Lucky old you! (*She stops.*) Yeah, yeah, I know. Sorry. Vulgar behaviour like that, that's what makes me so impossible. But it's no big deal. Just my happy disposition that's all. You should have thought of it sooner.

SLEEPWOMAN: What do you want with me?

IMPATIENT WOMAN: Can't you guess?

SLEEPWOMAN: I can't be bothered.

IMPATIENT WOMAN: Then I can go now.

SLEEPWOMAN: Please do.

IMPATIENT WOMAN: Oh yes, that would suit you, wouldn't it? Then you could move up one. I wouldn't do you that favour. We'll all stay, each in our place. Cramps your style, does it?

SLEEPWOMAN: Who are you anyhow?

IMPATIENT WOMAN: Well, while we're on the subject, yes, good question, who am I? I think you must be the only person who can help me find a satisfactory answer to that question.

SLEEPWOMAN: Give me a break will you?

IMPATIENT WOMAN: You don't know, do you, why you don't like me. But you're absolutely right not to like. I could tell you what your reasons are, but, well, you're probably not that interested…

OLAF: Well, I get up early, get dressed, make coffee, water the flowers, go shopping, make more coffee, get undressed again, go back to bed. I'm apathetic, I have no courage, no ambition, no lifestyle. I'm not even identifiable as the typical apathetic sort. Nor do I represent an exciting modern reinterpretation of traditional apathy. I am neither the first born nor the last born of the insatiable, unchangeable Goddess Apathie, conqueror of heaven and earth, who will tolerate no other heroes anywhere near her. I'm an expert on the history of apathy. I am its first chronicler and top expert, yet in no fibre of my being am I in any way, shape, or form, different from all the thousands and thousands of apathetic men there have ever been or ever will be.

In the evening, sometimes, when I put my trousers in the trouser press, I think: the day could well come when this mysterious tidiness in all things domestic, for which I am alone responsible, could just flip over into complete and utter chaos. This whole great big nice clean neat way of living, this whole cosmos of getting dressed, getting washed and particularly closing of cupboards when you have finished with them could just suddenly implode... A buckled, broken thing, it would creep under the carpet and hide while shameless, boundless, wallowing total bloody negligence, filth and leaving open of cupboards spreads its black leathery wings and terrorises the land. One shock too many, one more loveless encounter and I'll just let everything go: Hands wave service goodbye, senses remain quite unalarmed by the bad smell, the stain on the upholstery. It doesn't impinge. Let it stream over me. Let garbage and decay, newspapers and cigarette ends reach the sky, let blindness seep through filthy window panes, let coat hooks be festooned with dried up half-eaten sandwiches, for all I care.

JULIUS: Nobody asked you who you are, Olaf. Nobody asked!

OLAF: Really? Oh dear, I could have sworn I heard someone... No one asked me?! Can this be possible?! So why didn't anyone interrupt me? Why didn't anyone say anything? For God's sake – I made an effort. I came out of my shell – it's not fair.

JULIUS: All that stuff about your apathy, it could just as easily have applied to your touchiness.

(*Through the door stage right, MARIE STEUBER and the MAN WITH NO WATCH return.*)

IMPATIENT WOMAN: Oh, hello, wandered back from history have we? Back from your magical history tour? Did you arrive back at the year dot? Great man, isn't he?

MARIE STEUBER: A great man indeed.

IMPATIENT WOMAN: With a great mind.

MARIE STEUBER: Yes, that too.

IMPATIENT WOMAN: But, don't you think, a bit of a con-artist?

MARIE STEUBER: A bit. Doesn't matter though.

IMPATIENT WOMAN: No. Doesn't matter. You're absolutely right.

(*MARIE STEUBER leans up against the pillar. IMPATIENT WOMAN comes to her.*)

I was horrified seeing you again just now. When you came through the door. I thought, God, how coarse her features have become, how cold, how calculating, those deep deep lines around your mouth, your nose. Marie – what happened to your happy, smiling face? Your naïve jollity, your idle curiosity, your pointless little concerns, your lustfulness, your warmth, your full store of unspeakable but oh-so-loveable character defects? Everything about you's got so hard. So self-aware you've become, so tortured. And you've got horribly thin. Honestly, I could weep. It's as if a Hindu Goddess had lost her smile, as if all the wisdom of love…

(*MARIE STEUBER has disappeared into the pillar. We hear a key turning in the lock of the main door.*)

JULIUS: Pst! Sh!

(*Everyone listens to the door and everyone tests each other on their names.*)

Olaf?

OLAF: Yes?

SLEEPWOMAN: Ansgar?

MAN WITH NO WATCH: Yes?

IMPATIENT WOMAN: Julius?

JULIUS: Yes?

MAN WITH NO WATCH: Sabine?

IMPATIENT WOMAN: Yes?

OLAF: Dinah?

SLEEPWOMAN: Yes?

(*They all look around, asking, softly, 'Marie?' Through the door to the flat, bags and cases are pushed on.*)

Blackout.

Act Two

SCENE 1

The room. In the left corner a small pile of disposable lighters. Door opens. Luggage is pushed into the room. STEUBER and FRANK ARNOLD enter.

FRANK ARNOLD: Come in, please. Take your coat off. Have a seat. Can you I get you a drink? What would you like? Glass of whisky, wine, coffee?

MARIE STEUBER: Spot of wine would be lovely.

FRANK ARNOLD: Was the journey all right?

MARIE STEUBER: Yes, fine.

FRANK ARNOLD: Do you want to put your feet up for a bit? Or would you prefer to have a little wander through town?

MARIE STEUBER: Yes, that'd be great.

FRANK ARNOLD: Actually it's getting quite late. The shops'll be shut soon. Perhaps we'll wait till tomorrow morning. You can freshen up a bit here then in, what, a couple of hours, we could drive up to the castle – there's a good restaurant, with a fantastic view of the town. We could have supper there if that suits you.

MARIE STEUBER: Yes, lovely.

FRANK ARNOLD: But first, a drink. Cheers – and welcome.

MARIE STEUBER: Thanks, glad to be here.

FRANK ARNOLD: I can't tell you how relieved I am that you are here. Because I was late I was convinced we were going to miss each other at the airport.

MARIE STEUBER: Yes, me too, I'm glad it all worked out though I had to keep postponing the journey, putting it off. There was always something that cropped up and got in the way. But now that's all behind me, thank God, and I can get used to my new surroundings.

FRANK ARNOLD: I hope you won't regret having come here. I hope you'll find it relaxing. There's loads of room. You can just make yourself as comfortable as you can, wherever you like. The only possible fly in the ointment would be, well, me, I suppose.

MARIE STEUBER: How could you be a fly in the ointment? You're the reason I came.

FRANK ARNOLD: Well, do you think you'll be happy here?

MARIE STEUBER: I'm sure I will.

FRANK ARNOLD: I'm sometimes a bit, you know, impetuous. I suppose you'll have to get used to that. You're very – how shall I put it? Very friendly. Or, at least, that's how you come across.

MARIE STEUBER: Listen, that's fine. I get along with people very easily. My weaknesses lie elsewhere.

FRANK ARNOLD: Another drink?

MARIE STEUBER: Yes. Lovely.

FRANK ARNOLD: It won't be particularly easy. Possibly. I mean you're a very beautiful woman and after all, I'm only flesh and blood.

MARIE STEUBER: Well, that's as it should be.

FRANK ARNOLD: You're not worried about, you know, complications?

MARIE STEUBER: What could be complicated?

FRANK ARNOLD: What a question…look, you could always sleep in my bedroom; it's more comfortable, more space, um…

MARIE STEUBER: Yes, that'd be lovely.

FRANK ARNOLD: Just like that? Without even knowing me?

MARIE STEUBER: I haven't really thought about it yet.

FRANK ARNOLD: So you came here wanting to – this is what you want?

MARIE STEUBER: I didn't think about it. But now I'm here and all the other stuff, the ghastly stuff, is behind me, I'm ready to experience something new.

FRANK ARNOLD: I'm feeling, now, I'm feeling very excited by all this.

MARIE STEUBER: You know you look a bit unhealthy.

FRANK ARNOLD: Me, no, I –

MARIE STEUBER: I'm just saying it at the outset, so later you don't think I concealed anything.

FRANK ARNOLD: You mean, my face? This brittle old mask? This agony – can you see it?

MARIE STEUBER: Yes, it's all fine.

FRANK ARNOLD: Come here…

> (*They exit with their luggage, right, into the next room.*
> *Before the door is completely closed it is pushed open roughly.*
> *MARIE STEUBER and RUDOLPH enter.*)

SCENE 2

MARIE STEUBER: (*Against the wall.*) She is right! Right! Right!
Medea was right!

RUDOLPH: You have no cause to compare yourself to Medea.
We haven't got any children – I haven't deserted you for
the Princess Arouse, and yet you still seem to be turning
into her, into that monster.

MARIE STEUBER: She isn't a monster. She's just miserable, as
miserable as hell.

RUDOLPH: And are you?

MARIE STEUBER: Medea is very uncomplicated. Very natural.
Very primeval. Her world has fallen apart.

RUDOLPH: Excuse me but that doesn't give her the right to
sacrifice her children.

MARIE STEUBER: Doesn't give her the right! And what do
you know?! Not give her the right! Of course it does. She
loves Jason, more than anything in the world. And think
of everything they've been through together, how they've
suffered together. And how base it was of him to deceive
her.

RUDOLPH: Okay but I don't see the connection with you
and me. Tell me. What's the connection between you and
me on the one hand, and Jason and Medea on the other.
Where is it? Eh? Actually it's beginning to worry me a bit
the way this work of literature is going to your head. You'd
never read anything before. All you know is *Medea*, that's
all you've ever read.

MARIE STEUBER: I have no need to read anything else.

RUDOLPH: Read *Anna Karenina* or *Camille* or some other
profound and moving tale of woman's destiny.

MARIE STEUBER: Medea does everything in her power to
avoid disaster. But Jason doesn't listen.

RUDOLPH: Why should he listen? They're stuck in a Tragedy, for God's sake. Nothing they can do about it. But we're not are we? Stuck in a tragedy? There's no room for Medea in our life – there's no room for her, do you understand?

MARIE STEUBER: Medea commits the greatest act of love a woman has ever committed…

RUDOLPH: Yes – out of jealousy, out of pure selfishness. A desire to murder and destroy. You call that greatness?

MARIE STEUBER: Well – you're certainly no match for Jason. How can you say all that? Where did you get it from? Out of a book?

RUDOLPH: I don't know, I remember it from somewhere – I think I've got it right.

MARIE STEUBER: That play teaches us everything we need to know.

RUDOLPH: You should study literature – and then you'd learn how to read a play properly. It's dangerous to read a play, especially a tragedy, without really knowing what's what. In any drama there are always two protagonists with two points of view, and they're always both right – otherwise there'd be no drama. Everyone knows that from school.

MARIE STEUBER: So tell me in what way was Jason right? How was he right? To pillage, to slaughter, to destroy, to massacre. Blood! Blood! And a traitor to boot.

RUDOLPH: Fair enough. Matter of opinion.

MARIE STEUBER: Opinion? It's nothing to do with opinions. It's about emotions, eternal emotions, so great, so royal, so royal, so proud and black and strong and strange and EVERYTHING.

RUDOLPH: You're a big fan of this Medea of Kolchos.

MARIE STEUBER: Yes. I am. I am.

RUDOLPH: Fine. There are religious fanatics, political fanatics, sports fanatics etc. And they all make me sick. They're all idiots and that's that.

MARIE STEUBER: What about if someone's fanatically in love with you?

RUDOLPH: I have no need to be loved fanatically. I wouldn't demand that of anybody.

MARIE STEUBER: That's just what Medea can't understand.
That's the attitude she can't understand. Impossible. The
End. Blood and Fire.

RUDOLPH: I'd better confiscate the book. Away with tragedy.
I'll chuck in out into the street.

MARIE STEUBER: You don't seem to appreciate that Medea is
there. Always there. Demanding her rights. That we can't
just behave as if she didn't exist. No point in pushing her
away. Don't play silly games with thoughts and ideas. Try
and be smarter than Jason.

(*MARIE STEUBER leans against the pillar and looks out of the
window leaning against the pillar.*)

SCENE 3

MARIE STEUBER: I live here in the middle of the town and
in the middle of the roaring traffic. I'm surrounded by the
empty silent spaces in which nobody is really at home. Not
even my bread, my table, my radio, my sugar bowl. We've
all simply been forgotten, left here, abandoned here. No
one's got round to tidying us up. Someone's rushed off in
a hurry, and left us here, my stuff and me, just as passive,
as timeless as my table. My sugar bowl, my radio. I hear, I
stay.

PILLAR: Year in, year out, deeper and deeper. By as much as
the happy grow.

MARIE STEUBER: You can talk. How can you talk?

PILLAR: Everything speaks. I too speak.

MARIE STEUBER: Do not speak.

PILLAR: When you are silent for so long – you cannot find the
right words straight away.

MARIE STEUBER: The right words? No words, please. Do not
speak. You are my refuge. I want your silence. You are
the object I am leaning against because all my strength
has deserted me. Do not drive me from you with all this
speaky-speaky nonsense

PILLAR: Too late…

MARIE STEUBER: All these years you stayed silent? Said nothing?

PILLAR: That's right.

MARIE STEUBER: You'd always known the answer – but still you said nothing? So it was always voluntary silence – and not the dead silence of silent things – the ultimate silence.

PILLAR: I am pillar, I am column. I am a noun. I am masculine, feminine – it is painful. But now I have tried it. I found the sound. I was inside the words. It was purgatory.

MARIE STEUBER: You know much of my sadness. But now a disaster has happened.

PILLAR: Forgive me, will you. I have been banished from the heart of things.

MARIE STEUBER: Year in year out, deeper and deeper. By as much as the happy grow.

SCENE 4

The MAN WITH NO WATCH (ANSGAR) has been invited to MARIE STEUBER's. They're at supper.

ANSGAR: You're so beautiful – with your neat curly blond hair and you've invited a man to supper who's pug-ugly with thick spectacles, sweaty, clammy, smelly, a hypochondriac, a fat horrible slob and you're mocking me, you're laughing at me; you've even, I can't help noticing, slipped some sort of present, some gift under my serviette.

MARIE STEUBER: Yes it's just a little something for you. A memento of the day we met – last week.

ANSGAR: Thanks. (*He puts the present, unopened to one side.*) So. What's all this about? You're after that job aren't you? If you are, say so.

MARIE STEUBER: What job?

ANSGAR: Do you want the job or not?

MARIE STEUBER: I don't know what job you're talking about. I don't need a job – I haven't got a job but I don't need a job. I give you a present, I ring you up, because I don't seem to be able to forget our meeting at the trade fair, last week, when we talked for such a long time. And, okay, yes, perhaps I've fallen in love. I don't know what's the matter with you. If I'm a drag or a hassle just say so. I'm trying to get through to you, you understand, and I don't think

I can bear it any more – your secretary blocks my calls and obviously I can't phone you at home, so what am I supposed to do? I don't understand you at all.

ANSGAR: Thousands of people work in sales. You ought to set your sights on something more specific. Also vis-à-vis me. You have to know exactly what you want. It's absurd to just invite someone as repulsive as me to supper, just like that, I mean, come on, pull the other one – it's absurd.

MARIE STEUBER: It is absurd but you know I'll tell what's absurd, this is absurd: when a man like you says he's ugly, repulsive and all the rest of it.

ANSGAR: And a spectacle-wearer. Allow me that.

MARIE STEUBER: Absurd! I'm falling in love with you – God knows why.

ANSGAR: Quite.

MARIE STEUBER: Open your present.

ANSGAR: Take smaller mouthfuls, will you. I hate women who eat like that.

MARIE STEUBER: Stripped quite naked.

ANSGAR: Why? You?

MARIE STEUBER: Oh, well.

ANSGAR: Look to come to the point, that job you're so keen on went ages ago.

MARIE STEUBER: I don't give a fuck about your job. I don't want your job. I want you, Ansgar.
(*Pause.*)

ANSGAR: We only stuff our gobs so we stink all the more.

MARIE STEUBER: If you say so.

ANSGAR: Have you gone completely mad?

MARIE STEUBER: (*Over the glass which she's holding by the rim, leaning forward.*) I love you. Yes. I love you.

ANSGAR: Well. Okay. I think you're nice looking. You've got a sweet face – and the sort of tits I like. I mean okay. I think you're nice looking – but that's about it.

MARIE STEUBER: Do what you want – do whatever you want with me.

ANSGAR: Listen, if I wangle that job for you, then it's over one way or another. I have to keep my hands clean.

MARIE STEUBER: Stop it. Drop it. Look, now the whole thing's got this far we can see it's all madness anyway. Did it cross your mind what might happen if, you know, we had a few drinks and made ourselves comfortable and snuggly and nice.

ANSGAR: Yes, it crossed my mind on the way here.

MARIE STEUBER: And?

ANSGAR: I'd beat you up – if you pushed me that far I'd beat the shit out of you.

MARIE STEUBER: I don't know how I'm supposed to react to that – but to be honest, it's a bit of a turn-on.

ANSGAR: Shut your mouth! Who are you? How can anyone stoop so low? You're not just a man trap, a woman, so don't act like it, you're a human being. So stop this stupid bloody nonsense. Where's your dignity? Throw me out. Be proud. You disgust me.

MARIE STEUBER: Whatever you say – you'll still be waiting for me.

ANSGAR: No, hang on. Don't get up. You're a silly bitch. No let's find a good word to say for each other. Somehow.

MARIE STEUBER: I wouldn't dream of it.

ANSGAR: I could just snap my fingers, and then you'd be dreaming of it soon enough.

MARIE STEUBER: Please, do it.

ANSGAR: Don't start.

MARIE STEUBER: You've got this far – you've got no choice.

ANSGAR: Okay, let's drink this grappa – if we're going to have to, then I'm off.

MARIE STEUBER: (*Slaps the table.*) No!

ANSGAR: There's no job any more. Do you understand? It's taken.

MARIE STEUBER: Who got it?

ANSGAR: Some woman applied, I don't know. How should I know? I couldn't give a fuck.

MARIE STEUBER: (*Stamping her feet.*) I'm not interested. I'm not bloody interested, okay?

ANSGAR: Hey, hey, relax. Look, you've been making quite a fuss of me. I turn up here this evening obviously hoping that things will... So obviously I'm disappointed...

MARIE STEUBER: But I don't want to disappoint you.

ANSGAR: (*Smiles.*) You know I'm so ugly, so indescribably ugly that it's very easy for me to see if people are interested in me or in the ridiculously small amount of power I wield…

MARIE STEUBER: You're not, you're not.

ANSGAR: What, ugly or powerful?

MARIE STEUBER: Neither. Neither. I can't bear it. I can't bear it any more.

ANSGAR: Hey, little girl – what's your name again, what's your name?

MARIE STEUBER: Marie Steuber.

ANSGAR: Hey, Marie Steuber, don't go all floppy on me. Be strong. Come here. I don't want to play the big bad doctor. I just want some fun with you.

MARIE STEUBER: You don't need it. You don't need it any more.

ANSGAR: Marie Steuber!

MARIE STEUBER: No, let's stop this. No more grappa. I feel sick.

ANSGAR: Fine. I'll leave you to yourself, Marie.

MARIE STEUBER: Marie – how lovely that sounds. Like I'm hearing my name for the first time.

(*ANSGAR slaps her face with his napkin.*
MARIE jumps up, astonished.)

ANSGAR: Look, I'll say one thing. You've got the job – it's yours. Whether you like it or not. You've got the job. The job – but nothing but the job.

MARIE STEUBER: And I'll say one thing. You've got me – me and nothing but me.

SCENE 5

Three men in the reception room of an office. FRANK ARNOLD (FIRST MAN), the COMPLETE STRANGER (SECOND MAN), MAN IN THE WINTER COAT (THIRD MAN).

FIRST MAN: You being interviewed by a woman, who'd have thought it?

SECOND MAN: You're doing it too.

FIRST MAN: Yes, me, fair enough, but you! You're really big-time compared to me.

THIRD MAN: (*To SECOND MAN.*) You could've been the new Markus Bentheim. You had it in you.

FIRST MAN: Markus Bentheim, nothing. He could've been the new Jo Packart. The new Dieter Nabel. The new Albert Schneider. That's who he could've been.

SECOND MAN: I always kept my Sundays free. Free for the family. I never put my career first.

FIRST MAN: And look what's happened. Run at half power you'll never even cover half the distance. You'll always be lagging behind. Half power is worse than no power at all.

SECOND MAN: Oh, do leave off. Did you see that guy on the telly yesterday who blew out two hundred and fifty birthday candles with one puff?

FIRST MAN: That's absurd. And a meaningless achievement. I mean, who's going to get to their two hundred and fiftieth birthday?

SECOND MAN: You don't understand – it was a bet, a challenge. It's one of those programmes, you know, where people are set challenges. It's on every week.

THIRD MAN: Yes, I know, I've seen it. But two hundred and fifty years old, two hundred and fifty birthday candles – that's absurd.

FIRST MAN: Okay, it's absurd. Fine. But people enjoy it. That's the main thing. And apart from that I think it's also rather wonderful that someone's got such amazing long breath.

SECOND MAN: You obviously didn't see the show. It wasn't long, it was one short blast. And obviously a very powerful one. Very, very powerful. More like a hurricane! Two hundred and fifty lights, each one a life, what, four, five generations…

THIRD MAN: Sorry, it all sounds highly improbable.

FIRST MAN: Do you think he was cheating?

SECOND MAN: They never cheat on that programme.

FIRST MAN: That's what you think – they can bamboozle you in any number of ways.

SECOND MAN: If this programme, which you've plainly never seen…

FIRST MAN: I know exactly what sort of show it is.

SECOND MAN: If they started cheating on this programme, then it would be completely pointless. If they cheated, just once, by accident even, then the whole series would just collapse. It'd be over – like it never existed – snuffed out.

THIRD MAN: Like the candles. No I've got it. They built an invisible switch in the two hundred and fifty candles which snuffs them electronically.

SECOND MAN: That's absurd. I'm sorry but your view of this series is completely absurd.

EXECUTIVE: (*Leaning against the door.*) I'm very happy just to listen to whatever it is you gentlemen have got to say.

SCENE 6

MARIE STEUBER in her flat – about to set off. She's just finishing packing. A buzzer sounds. She opens the door. Enter OLAF also with travelling bags and cases.

MARIE STEUBER: Oh, is that you?

OLAF: Yes, me. Had you given up on me?

MARIE STEUBER: No – not at all – I was expecting, you know, someone a bit smaller. Wolfgang told me you wanted to stay here for as long as I'm away. I'm not sure you'll fit in my bed! You're awfully late – I was expecting you an hour ago – now I've got to go myself. Now, what do you need to know? Quick, quick, quick. Gas central heating – you know all about that, do you? You do? Good. Then, plants need watering every other day. Newspapers, post – you need to take out of the letter box downstairs – here's the little key for that. So – what a lot of responsibilities you've got! You won't be able to relax for a moment will you? Help yourself to whatever you need – this will be your flat for the next three months. I hope you'll be happy here… Oh, I'd love to be able to sit down and chat. We don't know each other at all. What a pity. And when I get back you'll have been long gone. And you must be very careful 'cause the toaster sticks a bit, doesn't pop up, that's if you want to make toast… I've got to go. So – farewell – make yourself at home. Perhaps you'll think of me now and then, as you sit here in my little fiat.

OLAF: Wait a moment. I haven't told you how pretty your
pictures are. They are yours, aren't they? You did them?

MARIE STEUBER: Yes. Do you like them? I'm not a serious...
I just dabble a bit. That's my sister with my ex...my ex-
boyfriend, I suppose.

OLAF: Oh, another thing. How do I pay for the telephone?

MARIE STEUBER: The telephone? Do you use it a lot? Write
it down somewhere. Or get people to ring you. Oh, you
know, do whatever suits you. Ring up your thousands
of girlfriends, feel free. No, hang on, something else,
very important, next month you need to book a window
cleaner. I'll leave you the money.

OLAF: No, please, I'll do that.

MARIE STEUBER: We'll settle up.

OLAF: We'll never see each other again, I'll pay.

MARIE STEUBER: Now, what else? What else is there?

OLAF: Yes, what else? I can't think of anything else.

MARIE STEUBER: Nothing else you want to ask me? My God
I've locked the cupboard. Now why did I do that?
(*She unlocks everything – the drawers in the cupboard and the
desk.*)
There we go – there we are. All yours!

OLAF: Why are you going?

MARIE STEUBER: I don't want to go. I don't want to at all.

OLAF: Then stay. Stay here.

MARIE STEUBER: No. I really must go. I must. Farewell.

OLAF: (*Almost shouts.*) The key to the cellar!

MARIE STEUBER: (*Jubilantly.*) The key to the cellar. Yes the
key to the cellar! I don't know where it is. I haven't the
faintest idea where I've put it. Yes, we've got to find it. Now
let's look for it, look for the key, look for the key.

OLAF: Do I actually need it?

MARIE STEUBER: Of course you need it. You absolutely need
it. No, you must ride my bicycle – otherwise it'll rust to
bits. (*She rummages around in the cupboard.*) Here's my photo
album – you must take a look at it. No. I won't let you. I'm
embarrassed. I'm always embarrassed, but why should I
be? No, it's fine – you should be getting a picture of the

person who lives here – but who isn't here – while you're living here. Look, that's me on my school trip into the mountains – no, you must look at them in your own good time. Promise? Obviously the key isn't in the cupboard. Obviously. No the key is on top of the cupboard. (*She gets on a chair.*) Here is the key to the cellar. And up here there's letters. A bundle of letters. Secret letters. Bad, naughty letters. Which you're not to read. Which you absolutely, definitely mustn't read. You promise? (*She leaves the letters in an obvious place, behind the glass door in the top part of the cupboard, she locks it and places the key on the sideboard.*) Never! Right, so let's say I stayed. And you never went to work. And I never got out of this place. Out of myself. Out of this rut.

OLAF: If you stayed and I stayed – everything would be different here. It'd be just as new for you as for me.

MARIE STEUBER: No. I'm going.

OLAF: I'll come with you.

MARIE STEUBER: Your work!

OLAF: You're right. I can't. I'll stay here.

MARIE STEUBER: Why are we such indecisive people?!

OLAF: There's always that moment hanging in the air – when everything could go one way – or another.
(*A ring at the door.*)

MARIE STEUBER: The taxi! Will you help me down with my suitcases?

OLAF: I will do no such thing. You're staying here.

MARIE STEUBER: No. Too late. You could have simply taken me, taken me in your arms. And everything would have turned out differently.

OLAF: Was it only up to me?

MARIE STEUBER: I don't know. I wasn't feeling so sure of myself either.

OLAF: Now I'll just have to stay here in your flat and think of you.

MARIE STEUBER: And I'll just have to think of you here in my flat.

OLAF: No, when you're travelling you'll be distracted thinking of something else. You travel, you forget.

MARIE STEUBER: Imagine if I hadn't gone – If I'd stayed. We'd be standing here looking at each other, rather self-consciously.

OLAF: It would have been a big big decision. A big responsibility. We'd've had to somehow justify it.

MARIE STEUBER: Quite. Just suddenly – and forever.

OLAF: But now? What's now?

MARIE STEUBER: Now? Now don't forget to take good care of my washing machine. I don't have any house insurance. So no little disasters please. And when you go again, when you leave, shut all the windows, turn off all the taps, switch off the fridge, take the rubbish out, strip down the beds, don't leave any money lying around, turn all the lights off, pop the keys into the letter box, don't leave any trace...
(*She's leaning against his shoulder.*
Blackout.)

SCENE 7

OLAF sitting at the window. JULIUS enters by the door stage right.

JULIUS: Right. So – what's on the agenda?

OLAF: Nothing.

JULIUS: (*Sits on the chair facing into the room.*) I'm just the way I am. Which doesn't seem to suit you particularly.

OLAF: You know I have my own specific energy, but your endless wringing your hands, your inability to face up to the universal emptiness of everything is almost unbearable.

JULIUS: It was your idea that I should come and live with you.

OLAF: Yeah. Perhaps it wasn't that brilliant an idea.

JULIUS: But you give the impression of wanting to meet people, you seem genuinely interested –

OLAF: I am – but on the other hand I can only rely on myself – and I need my own peace and quiet.

JULIUS: Well, I'll say it again, I didn't force myself on you.

OLAF: No, of course you didn't. It's fine.

JULIUS: Don't go. Sit here with me for a bit, just a bit.

OLAF: My former wife.

JULIUS: A radiant beauty.

OLAF: No, she wasn't that. Just occasionally she got her act together enough to look sort of okay. No she was fine. But her shoulders were too narrow, her face too small, her hair too thin…

JULIUS: A very winning personality.

OLAF: No she wasn't that. She was more – coy, almost cold. But with a bit of help – bit of polish, she was fine.

JULIUS: A lively, cheerful person.

OLAF: A very sad human being. And when I see how miserable Marie is now, trying desperately to get some semblance of order in her life…

JULIUS: That's just awful.

OLAF: Oh no, it's not that awful.

(*Telephone next door.*)

JULIUS: Are you going?

OLAF: No, you go.

(*JULIUS exits through the door stage right. OLAF gets up, goes to the window.*)

The Christmas trees are still lying at the sides of the road and it's February. Heaps of sand fringed by tongues of ice like plastic leaves. (*He smiles.*) Girls give a quick glance at their reflections in the shop windows, give their hair a quick brush as they scurry past… (*He sits down on the seat facing the room.*) In spite of everything I'm glad he still pops a cigarette in his mouth as soon he comes in through the door. It shows that he's still a little bit excited. It shows he hasn't gone completely apathetic.

(*JULIUS enters by the right-hand door. Lights a cigarette, sits in the chair by the window.*)

Who was it?

JULIUS: Ansgar.

OLAF: And? Did he say 'hello' to me?

JULIUS: No, he forgot.

OLAF: Oh, he forgot. So I'm nothing to him.

JULIUS: Now don't go all moody again.

OLAF: Why can't he spare a thought, a single word for me? He knows full well how delighted I am when someone says 'hello' – even as an afterthought, even absent-mindedly.

JULIUS: Frequently he's said, 'Say hello to Olaf for me,' and you couldn't've cared less.

OLAF: No. I could never not have cared less.

JULIUS: Oh, come on. It meant nothing to you. You didn't give a toss. Didn't even react. And now suddenly when he overlooks you – you have a nervous breakdown.

OLAF: It's just a bit much. That's all.

JULIUS: But whether he says 'hello' or doesn't say 'hello', I mean it's not the end of the world.

OLAF: That depends entirely on the balance of one's mind, doesn't it? In some circumstances to forget to say 'hello' is just the thin end of the wedge. Anyway, you could have protected me from this latest trauma by just saying, 'Oh, by the way Ansgar said to say "hello",' in spite of the painful fact that he quite palpably didn't. Just in the interests of a quiet life you could've done that. It would have been a matter of sensitivity. A nice gesture.

JULIUS: I could never do that.

OLAF: Your rigorous sense of propriety takes no account of other people's feelings. You're quite happy to stand there and watch my spirits plummet rather than jollying me along with a harmless little lie of convenience.

JULIUS: Look, I'm afraid the result of your endlessly picking away at this particular scab is that now, if he should ring again and if he really says, 'Oh, say hello to Olaf for me,' and I say, 'Oh by the way Ansgar said "hello",' then you won't believe me and you'll tell me (you will, I know you) that it's just a 'lie of convenience' designed to spare your feelings (because now I know how much it matters to you, and what you really want to hear) that I'll just tell you what you want to hear whether it's true or not – but you'll never, ever really know whether he really said to say 'hello' or whether I'm just saying that he said 'hello' to spare your feelings.

OLAF: Well, I suppose this had to happen sooner or later. You pushed things to the brink with your smug sense of right and wrong.

JULIUS: What do you mean I have? You have. If you hadn't brought up the subject of lies of convenience then we wouldn't be having the slightest problem with all this did he say 'hello' or not nonsense.

OLAF: Okay, but say one time, like just now, he *didn't* say to say 'hello' and you fraudulently say, 'Oh by the way Ansgar says "hello",' then couldn't you say it in a slightly higher voice and screw up your left eye. Then I'd know, and then the shock would be slightly dissipated.

JULIUS: Then we'd be back to square one. I mean what's the difference between a glaringly obvious lie, a high-pitched voice lie that wrinkles the face, which screws up the eye and the naked truth, the harsh reality?

OLAF: The reality of the matter is in this particular case neither here nor there. It's much more important that you've considered me, and made some sort of effort on the one hand to spare my feelings but on the other to make it vaguely clear, or rather precisely clear to me that you're giving me a sign, being a little attentive, providing a bit of fun, a bit of make-believe, in order to ease the tension between us, to give a sense of playfulness, because as far as I'm concerned, whether he actually said, 'Say hello to Olaf' or he didn't say, 'Say hello to Olaf' is a matter of complete indifference as long as you *care* – as long as it means something to you whether I'm indifferent or unindifferent or different or whatever, and if I can therefore feel that it's somehow brought us closer together then it'd be as if lies and reality never existed and the gloom which always descends over me after those sorts of phone calls, which is now let's face it all the deeper 'cause now I'll never *really* know whether he said to say 'hello' or didn't say to say 'hello' even if you do screw up your eye, even if you don't (who cares, do what you like), the whole depression of the whole bloody business would be just the tiniest bit alleviated. That's all. That's all I ask.

SCENE 8

A reception room to an office, which is reached through the right-hand door. At the left window, which is open, a man is standing; he looks ill, breathing deeply. At the right window MARIE STEUBER eating pastry, drinking milk out of a carton. Right-hand door half open. Street noise, computers bleeping, telephones buzzing. From the door steps a fellow worker, the IMPATIENT WOMAN.

COLLEAGUE: I'll go in the lunch break Marie. Could you give the printer a quick buzz after one to see if Schmidt and Wolf have delivered the design proposals for the brochure?

MARIE STEUBER: Sure. Will do.

COLLEAGUE: Have you heard from Olaf?

MARIE STEUBER: Oh him. I asked him to go to Madrid with me for Easter. He sent me a video of him pouting. Just that. That's all I can get out of him!

COLLEAGUE: Why don't you consult your tarot cards again?

MARIE STEUBER: Yeah, maybe.

COLLEAGUE: See you later.

MARIE STEUBER: Have a good lunch.

> *(Exit COLLEAGUE through door, left. Soon after, enter a CUSTOMER – MAN IN WINTER COAT – and the SLEEPWOMAN who is the BOSS.)*

CUSTOMER: In our house it's very simple: the woman brings the culture into the home, the man deals with the money.

BOSS: Why not the other way round? The woman deals with the money, the man brings culture into the house.

CUSTOMER: Why do you have to turn everything on its head? What's the point?

BOSS: I know you – your ideal is a salesgirl in a shop: sits sweetly at your feet and asks if everything's okay. *(To MARIE STEUBER.)* Enjoy your lunch.

MARIE STEUBER: You too, Frau Siebwald.

> *(Both exit the door stage left. Enter GRAPHIC ARTIST/THE COMPLETE STRANGER.)*

GRAPHIC ARTIST: *(To MARIE STEUBER.)* I've just seen Schmidt and Wolf. Can I speak to Fraulein Dubbe?

MARIE STEUBER: She's just gone to lunch.

GRAPHIC ARTIST: I've got the proposals for the next year's brochure.

MARIE STEUBER: Oh, haven't they got to the printers yet? Why don't you leave them on her desk.

> *(GRAPHIC ARTIST exits. Comes straight back.)*

GRAPHIC ARTIST: Actually I'm in a bit of a rush. Could you tell her I'll ring her later. There's a couple of questions.

MARIE STEUBER: We've met before, haven't we?

GRAPHIC ARTIST: Yes. Indeed. How's things?

MARIE STEUBER: Fine. Yourself?

GRAPHIC ARTIST: Oh, you know...busy busy busy.

MARIE STEUBER: Still?

GRAPHIC ARTIST: Yes – doesn't stop. When was it we...?

MARIE STEUBER: It was, hang on, it was, September '82 at the Town Hall.

GRAPHIC ARTIST: September '82 – can't have been – I was in the States.

MARIE STEUBER: Are you sure? Or was it '83?

GRAPHIC ARTIST: At the Town Hall?

MARIE STEUBER: Yes – at the victory celebrations after the roadrace.

GRAPHIC ARTIST: I don't think it can have been me.

MARIE STEUBER: We know each other from somewhere, I think that's obvious.

GRAPHIC ARTIST: Yes... I think it goes back further than that.

MARIE STEUBER: Perhaps. I'm sure you're right. It must have been a long time ago.

GRAPHIC ARTIST: It's amazing how you can hang on to a face and forget everything else.

MARIE STEUBER: Absolutely everything else.

GRAPHIC ARTIST: Sorry – look I've got to go. Have a good day.

MARIE STEUBER: You too.

GRAPHIC ARTIST: What's the matter with him over there?

MARIE STEUBER: He's not well. Every hour or so he comes down from his office to gulp a bit of fresh air. They've got air-conditioning up there. You can't open the windows.

GRAPHIC ARTIST: Do you know who he is?

MARIE STEUBER: No.

GRAPHIC ARTIST: He looks like he's going to have a heart-attack. Perhaps we should call an ambulance? You never know whether you should help or not. Whether you should intervene. I think I'll give him a wide berth. I hate looking at that sort of thing. (*He turns to MARIE STEUBER.*) Look, tell me when it's over.

MARIE STEUBER: You know I really think you don't remember.

GRAPHIC ARTIST: I don't – do you?

MARIE STEUBER: I don't either. Alas. I can't get a fix on it. I'm racking my memory.

GRAPHIC ARTIST: Just too long ago.

MARIE STEUBER: But we still recognised each other. No trouble.

GRAPHIC ARTIST: And straight away too. Nice.

MARIE STEUBER: Well yes, nice, that's probably exactly what it was then, as far as I can tell. Perhaps it was as nice as nice could be. I just don't remember.

GRAPHIC ARTIST: Lost in the mists of time. But someone's face, it never really goes away.

MARIE STEUBER: You can turn round now. He's gone. He was only getting some air.

GRAPHIC ARTIST: I don't like people being ill – it makes me feel all funny.

MARIE STEUBER: It's all over now. You ought to go.

GRAPHIC ARTIST: Yeah I should. But listen – if I come straight back through the door, that means I've remembered something, okay?

MARIE STEUBER: Yes, absolutely. And if I come running up behind you, that means I've remembered something. All right?

GRAPHIC ARTIST: All right. Well then – see you soon, I hope.

MARIE STEUBER: You hope?

GRAPHIC ARTIST: Or never…

MARIE STEUBER: Whatever it was then can't have been that big a deal. Can't've been.

GRAPHIC ARTIST: Even so, I'd like to know – if it ever comes back to you. Have a good day.

MARIE STEUBER: Yeah. You too.

Blackout.

The End.

.